THE RELIGION BUSINESS

THE
RELIGION
BU$INESS

ALFRED BALK

JOHN KNOX PRESS
Richmond, Virginia

The author gratefully acknowledges permission from *Harper's* magazine to reprint portions of the text which appeared in his article "God Is Rich" (*Harper's*, October 1967).

When one remembers that churches pay no inheritance tax (churches do not die), that churches may own and operate business and be exempt from the 52 per cent corporate income tax, and that real property used for church purposes (which in some states are most generously construed) is tax exempt, it is not unreasonable to prophesy that with reasonably prudent management, the churches ought to be able to control the whole economy of the nation within the predictable future.

—Dr. Eugene Carson Blake
General Secretary,
World Council of Churches;
Former Stated Clerk,
United Presbyterian Church
in the U.S.A.

THE RELIGION BUSINESS

I

America's religious community is rich—richer than any counterpart in recent history; richer than even most ecclesiastical leaders in this country are willing to concede. Indeed, when Dr. Eugene Carson Blake's provocative statement quoted above was publicized, it not only shocked but angered many churchmen. But it is not a visionary forecast. American organized religion has become an economic behemoth and already, more than most devout local parishioners will allow themselves to admit, it has assumed the broad characteristics of a business—emulating the corporate-oriented administrative, financial, and public relations objectives of the marketplace. And the internal yardsticks by which its leaders most often measure its progress have become those of the marketplace.

Consider, first of all, some of the more conventional indexes of organized religion's financial power. As of the 1960 census, the Government reports, there were some 320,000 church parishes in the United States—or, corrected for a population of some 200 million and for new churches completed, one for approximately every 600 Americans. Every year, the National Council of Churches of Christ in the U.S.A. calculates, these parishes gather in contributions of about $5 billion—approximately half of all philanthropic giving in this country—and they invest more than $1 billion in new facilities. According to a study sponsored by Americans United for Separation of Church and State,* these religious organizations' "visible assets"—land and buildings of all kinds—now have a value of at least $79.5 billion: almost double the combined assets of the country's five largest industrial corporations. Of this treasure, approximately $44.5 billion worth is held by the Roman Catholic Church. These estimates have not been challenged. In fact, a Catholic priest, the Reverend Richard Ginder, writing in the Roman Catholic publication *Our Sunday Visitor,* said:

"The Catholic Church must be the biggest corporation in the United States. We have a branch office in almost every neighborhood. Our assets and real estate holdings must exceed those of Standard Oil, AT & T, and U.S. Steel combined. And our roster of dues-paying members must be second only to the tax rolls of the United States Government."

Denominational pension and retirement funds invested in stocks, bonds, and mortgages total more than $2 billion. Churches' consumption of materials and services, both for growing parish plants and for church-owned educational and welfare institutions, is gargantuan—the Roman Catholic archdiocese of New York City reportedly spent $17,000,000 on goods and services in its jurisdiction alone in a recent year. And a burgeoning financial field known as the "religious bond business" now involves, according to the president of one of the largest firms specializing in "religious" construction, "not millions but billions to be spent."

But in a big country, bigness of plant and payroll are, per se, neither inappropriate nor indicative of materialistic compulsions. It is only on closer analysis that one begins to

---

* *Church Wealth and Business Income,* Martin A. Larson (New York: Philosophical Library, 1965).

comprehend how thoroughly the institutional base of American organized religion has changed from the humbler period of the community parson and the small-town "meetin' house." Peter De Vries perhaps best depicted the change in his novel *The Mackeral Plaza,* in the description of the Peoples' Liberal Church of Avalon, Connecticut. The institution —"the first split-level church in America," its progressive young minister proudly proclaims—features an elaborate clinic for psychiatric treatment and an interior "convertible into an auditorium for putting on plays, a gymnasium for athletics, and a ballroom for dances. There is a small worship area at one end."

Today, the parish norm for American Protestants, Roman Catholics, and Jews alike is indeed the upholstered and, in many instances, the air-conditioned pew. And few sophisticated church trustees regard their parishes as adequately appointed if limited to a church sanctuary, Sunday school rooms, and a parsonage. The fashionable parish, Protestant or Catholic, fundamentalist or "modernist," also must—and usually does—have at least a "Christian education wing," a banquet and recreation complex, an auxiliary chapel, multiple parsonages for its multimember ministerial staff, one or more hard-surface parking lots, a vehicle fleet, and a woods-and-water recreation camp.

The physical plant of a Baptist church in Dallas, for instance, in addition to a sanctuary for worship, includes a seven-story parking and recreation building with skating rink, a gym, and four bowling lanes. And, in perhaps the ultimate manifestation of the phenomenon, a Protestant complex in West Palm Beach, Florida, known as Bibletown, U.S.A., consists of a 2,500-seat auditorium, two education buildings, employee quarters, parking lots, a motel used for retreats, mass dining facilities, and 15 acres of recreation area—including a swimming pool, tennis court, and shuffleboard courts.

Nor are European-style medieval-type cathedrals passé in this country. The Episcopal Cathedral of St. John the Divine, for example, long a popular tourist attraction in New York City, is second in size among churches only to St. Peter's in Rome. Dozens of other U.S. church edifices are only slightly smaller, including the massive National Shrine of the Immaculate Conception and the Washington Cathedral in Washington, D.C., and, in New York City, the multimillion-dollar St. Patrick's, which occupies a city block along one of the most expensive sections of Fifth Avenue in midtown Manhattan.

But the holdings of religious organizations nowadays are by no means limited to such benevolent undertakings as church sanctuaries, parsonages, schools, and welfare organizations. American sectarian groups also have taken deep plunges into profit-making businesses. In Los Angeles, the Temple Baptist Church owns the Philharmonic Auditorium and office building; the Muskingum, Ohio, Presbytery operates a cement-block factory—based in Arizona; California's Christian Brothers are major winemakers and one of the country's leading producers of brandy; and a Southern California sect, the Self-Realization Fellowship, operates a chain of eateries featuring Mushroomburgers.

The Mormon Church in Utah includes among its properties the Salt Lake City *Deseret News;* radio-TV station KSL; a department store; more than 100,000 acres of farm-ranch land (managed through a holding company, Zion Securities Corporation); and Laie Village in Honolulu, which *Variety* has called one of the best "potential tourist catchalls to be found on an island paradise already teeming with tourist bait." Large blocs of stock in Republic and National Steel corporations and in the Boeing, Lockheed, Curtiss-Wright, and Douglas aircraft companies are held by the Roman Catholic Jesuits. In addition, the same order has a substantial interest in the immense DiGiorgio Fruit Company, which operates in California, Florida, and Central America, and runs its own steamship fleet.

The $300 million assets of the Knights of Columbus—the Catholic fraternal, insurance, and evangelizing group—include a steel-tube factory, several department stores, and the land under Yankee Stadium in New York City. And in Washington, D.C., the entrepreneur for the new Watergate Project, a $70,000,000 commercial redevelopment enterprise adjacent to the John F. Kennedy Center for the Performing Arts, is the Societa Generale Immobiliare, mammoth Italian real estate company in which the Vatican—whose economic support derives substantially from American Roman Catholics—is the largest shareholder. Encompassing a choice 10-acre site near the Potomac, this ambitious enterprise will include hotel, shopping center, offices, and more than 1,000 luxury apartments.

Boasting the most ecumenical portfolio of all, however, is an Ohio Protestant group known as the Cathedral of Tomorrow—whose properties include a shopping center, an apartment building, an electronics firm, a wire and plastic company, and the Real Form Girdle Company. "A church owns Real Form? This is preposterous!" said the executive secretary of the Associated Corset and Brassiere Manufacturers when *Women's Wear Daily* disclosed this somewhat esoteric holding under the headline "ROCK OF AGES ON FIRM FOUNDATION." But the Reverend Rex Humbard, pastor of the Cathedral of Tomorrow, cheerfully acknowledged the fact.

"There is nothing unusual about our owning business firms," he said. "All churches do. What difference does it make if it's a girdle company or an airplane company?"

Few church leaders probably would be quite so permissive. On the other hand, even in some churches which retain strict scruples against profit-making corporate activities, it is not uncommon to find other striking refinements on biblical teachings. Steadily growing in influence, for example, are professional promotion and fund-raising counsel who—for a fee—help churches extract contributions from their own members; management seminars for ministers; and, in large and affluent parishes, a new permanent paid staff member with a title such as Church Business Manager. One of his jobs is to deal with the hordes of specialized equipment and supply firms—a sort of religious-industrial complex—which have sprung up solely to serve the physical needs of religious institutions. Perusing any of several ministerial, church equipment, or church business management magazines, one may find these firms candidly catering to, as well as helping create, demand for their wares with such advertisements as: (for a church organ) SPLENDOR WORTHY OF YOUR SERVICE, and (for a lightweight, prefabricated, rustproof aluminum church spire) A SYMBOLIC SPIRE, POINTING TO GOD, CRAFTED BY OVERLY.

Economically, then, organized religion is one of the nation's most vigorous growth industries, with a broadly based and expanding blue-chip portfolio, no union problems, an enviable tax status, and impressive strength in an area in which business analysts once regarded it as not only weak but unmotivated: its financial management. Once—but no more.

II

How have churches become so deeply immersed in materialistic endeavors?

Part of the answer lies in their tax status. From the time of ancient Egyptian kings, religion has received broad-based financial concessions from government. The early Osirian priesthood in Egypt annually received tax-exempt revenue amounting to one-third of the national income, and the Zoroastrian and Mandaean priests of Persia and the pre-Buddhist Brahmans in India enjoyed similar privileges. Under the Roman Emperor Constantine in the fourth century A.D., the church achieved even greater power and privileges than the ancients—all religious personnel were placed on the public payroll, church construction and maintenance were financed out of public funds, and the church in effect became a ruling partner of the state, eventually possessing about one-third of the real property of the Empire. A wave of expropriation of church property ultimately resulted, but in Germany, among other nations, churches still are financed partly from general revenues.

(This, a delegation from the Church of Hamburg blushingly noted some months ago, has placed organized religion in Germany in the bizarre position of subsisting partly on the tax contributions of such impious wage earners as prostitutes. The congregation's solution to this embarrassment: a request that church taxes no longer be levied on prostitutes.)

All of the original American colonies except Rhode Island at first flirted with a pattern of government-established religion. In the Massachusetts colony, for instance, an act of 1692 required every town to choose a minister by majority vote and to share in his support. When adherents of the Church of England protested against paying taxes to support other faiths, all professed members of the denomination were exempted from the general tax on public worship. The Quakers, whose religion allowed them no minister, also were granted exemption from the ministerial tax. Thus was established the principle of damping denominational struggles by granting all religious groups exemptions from taxes on property used for worship and, by extension, from taxes on other assets; gift and inheritance taxes; and from income taxes. Contributions to religious organizations also were made tax-exempt.

"By the time the Constitution and its Bill of Rights were written," Dr. Merrill D. Moore, executive secretary of the Stewardship Commission of the Southern Baptist Convention, noted in a study paper on the subject, "there had been enough experience of state church religious monopoly, oppressive religious taxes, domination by force of the lives of the citizens in the name of religion, that the leaders of the young nation had arrived at the decision that such evils must be eliminated and prevented from appearing in American life."

By the same rationale—the Constitutional imperative of separation of church and state—churches and religious groups, alone among nonprofit institutions, never have been required to file declarations of assets, income, or other financial dealings. Nor are bond issues in the name of religious organizations usually required to undergo normal governmental scrutiny, unless voluntarily submitted to securities agencies or of a magnitude and marketing pattern—rare among religious organizations—that requires the Securities and Exchange Commission's or state authorities' advance clearance. (Once there is a reasonable suspicion of irregularities, however—as in a series of alleged frauds the *Wall Street Journal* and other publications attributed to a small circle of promoters not long ago—government intervention may occur.) Further, to avoid entanglements in complex questions of church and state, courts and tax authorities have been chronically timid in defining legitimate religious activity and what constitutes a bonafide religion or religious group.

Given this favored economic position in a country of consistent economic and population growth, organized religion needed only two other elements to foster a "takeoff" in rapid amassing of wealth: (1) centralized management and (2) a motivation to exploit tax concessions to accelerate accumulation of assets. These institutional elements long have been present in Roman Catholicism—they were prime causes of the Reformation—and in such Protestant groups as the Church of England (whose wealth, despite its waning influence, now is so vast that it yields half the church's income and must be administered by a joint church-governmental Church Estates Commission). But only in this century has the U.S. branch of the Roman Catholic Church achieved a broad enough membership base to achieve domestic economic prominence, and only in recent decades has U.S. Protestantism, through natural growth, mergers, and expanding secularization, developed the requisites of acquisitiveness.

(Materialistic inclinations in American organized religion are not, of course, confined to the Christian churches. Elaborately designed and lavishly equipped synagogues abound. But, for the moment at least, Jewish religious organizations are not heavily involved in commerce. This may be because America's fewer than 6,000,000 Jews are not numerous or cohesive enough; or possibly because, through centuries of experience, they have learned that a religion grows too opulent at its own peril. In any event, because of these distinctions and because Judaism is so manifestly a minority faith in this country, the focus of this book is on the nation's organized Protestant and Catholic faiths.)

The history of one little-known tax anomaly is particularly instructive. The anomaly is a provision of the Internal Revenue Service Code granting churches and sacerdotal orders exemption from federal income tax on "unrelated business income"—income not directly derived from the statutory purpose for which a tax-exempt institution is chartered. Thus, if a church or other nonprofit religious organization is the owner of record, profits are tax-free whether or not the business is directly related to the owner's primary mission, and whether or not the church staff directly manages the profit-making enterprise.*

When the original federal income tax law was passed in 1913, all general charitable, educational, agricultural, scientific, literary, and fraternal organizations also were accorded this favorable tax treatment. Over the years, apparently with governmental blessing, many of these organizations sought to utilize their exemptions as ingeniously as do some religious organizations now. One of the most noteworthy examples was a New York University affiliate's acquisition of a spaghetti company's stock, and a request for an exemption from taxes on the firm's profits. A number of similar cases involv-

* Not all organizations mentioned in this book claim exemption from all taxes of all levels of government. The Knights of Columbus, for example, report that real estate taxes are paid on their behalf by the lessee of Yankee Stadium, among other properties. And the Christian Brothers Winery (De La Salle Institute), since losing a lawsuit within the past decade have paid substantial federal taxes; had the business been operated by the Jesuits, Franciscans, or some other religious order, however, it would have been exempt.

ing other institutions were publicized. Consequently, when hearings began in 1950 on the first over-all postwar revenue reform, federal tax exemptions for the unrelated business income of all nonprofit institutions—including religious organizations—came into question.

Here the distinction between the churches' traditionally privileged status and the position of other nonprofit institutions—as well as a conspicuous contrast between the attitudes of the hierarchies of American higher education and organized religion—were significantly revealed. Representatives of higher education in general supported the taxing of unrelated business income. "I cannot believe that it is sound public policy to exempt from federal taxation the income of manufacturing and commercial enterprises merely because they are owned by charitable institutions," said Paul C. Cabot, treasurer of Harvard University. "It is easy to see that two businesses that are directly competitive cannot in fact compete if one of them must pay . . . federal income tax and the other pay nothing." Added Dr. J. F. Killian, president of the Massachusetts Institute of Technology, who was representing the Association of American Universities: "I also feel that our colleges and universities have a responsibility not to engage in business or investment practices which might be reasonably judged to be borderline or outside the tax-exemption area."

There were no comparable statements—written or oral— from representatives of organized religion. Only one nationally prominent religious spokesman went on the record— A. B. Culbertson, vice president of the Baptist Foundation of Texas, which invests endowment funds of Texas Baptist institutions—this to plead for an amendment specifying that the pending bill not only exempt "a church" in the collective denominational sense, but also exempt autonomous churches, so that individual Baptist congregations (which, technically, are independent rather than being members of a central body) would not find their parish exemptions jeopardized. The requested amendment was approved, and the bill, signed into law, allowed religious organizations to retain the lucrative exemption on unrelated business income, as did a narrowly restricted group of certain nonprofit educational, social-welfare, and fraternal societies.

Why did Congress, in removing the exemption on unrelated business income from nonsectarian private schools and social agencies, among others, not also withdraw this privilege from churches?

"There was a staff proposal that did include churches," a representative of the Joint Congressional Committee on Internal Revenue taxation recalls. "The proposal would have treated churches as it treated other tax-exempt organizations in regard to unrelated business income. But it never became part of the bill."

Had church groups been consulted about this by Congressmen or their staffs?

"I don't think they were consulted. We knew that they would be opposed. It was a touchy question then. It is touchy now. Everybody is reluctant to do anything to suggest he is against religion."

This tax immunity on business ventures—by one governmental act suddenly a relatively rare prerogative of religious organizations—spurred their entry into a whole spectrum of business activities. In the process, many erstwhile private enterprises have been removed from the tax rolls, and serious problems have been created for tax-paying competitors. In Dayton, Ohio, for example, the president of a firm called Technology, Inc., complained that he had been underbid on a $500,000 Air Force contract because the winning bidder, the University of Dayton, is operated by the Roman Catholic Society of Mary and therefore is exempt from corporate income taxes. "The federal taxes we would have paid . . .

would have been much more than the $10,000 less the University of Dayton bid," he said. In New Orleans, another Roman Catholic institution, Loyola University, long has operated profitably (and tax-free) one of the city's three largest radio-TV stations, WWL and WWL-TV, a CBS affiliate.

"When I pay talent or buy feature film," said an executive of a competing TV station, "I've got to use after-tax dollars. They use before-tax dollars. If they spend $100,000 on promotion during rating periods, I need $200,000 to match it. The university and its station are good citizens in our community, but I can't believe this is a fair thing."

(As a profit-making arm of a religious order WWL does not, however, seem overpowered by its "good-citizen" responsibilities. By spring 1967, its evening programming in prime time consisted chiefly of movies; New Orleans viewers saw "CBS Reports"—the network's principal public-affairs series—only because the local educational station presented it on a delayed broadcast.)

Commercial enterprises as well as the churches have found such partnerships eminently advantageous, thanks to an arrangement known as a "sale and lease-back." The general procedure is this: a church or religious organization buys a business, financing the purchase with a mortgage. It then leases the plant back to the same operators. The church takes most of the earnings—perhaps as much as 80 percent—as rent on which it is now taxed—and thus pays off the mortgage in installments. In effect, the business buys itself. Since the church pays no taxes it can, of course, offer the original owner a higher price than an ordinary tax-paying purchaser. This is the moral of an article in a newsletter called *Executive Tax Report,* published by Prentice-Hall. "HAVE YOU PUT A PRICE ON YOUR BUSINESS?" "YOU MAY BE ABLE TO DOUBLE IT—BY SELLING TO A CHARITY." "An ordinary buyer," the article explains, "is interested only in earnings after taxes—that is all he gets to see. But a tax-exempt buyer keeps a hundred cents on the dollar. So a fair price for charity would be . . . twice what you figured."

Andrew D. Tanner, a Nashville attorney who conducted a study of church tax exemptions for the National Conference of Christians and Jews, estimates that a church can generally recover the entire cost of the property, plus interest, in no more than 20 years.

In 1953, the Knights of Columbus used the "sale and lease-back" technique to acquire the land under Yankee Stadium in a series of financial moves involving a Chicago broker. The same method enabled three Bloomington, Illinois, churches—the First Baptist, First Christian, and Second Presbyterian—to purchase the 435-room Biltmore Hotel in Dayton from the Hilton Hotels chain—without spending a penny of church money.

"Wealthy members pledged $200,000 in personal loans for the down payment," the *Wall Street Journal* noted. "The hotel was leased back to the chain with rent to be applied against interest rates and the balance of the debt. The hotel [since has been] transferred to its original owners. Profit to the churches: $450,000. Such 'lease-backs' are a favorite religious investing technique."

Under similar arrangements, the *Journal* reported, the Southern Baptist Annuity Board paid $2,900,000 for a Cheraw, South Carolina, textile mill and leased it back to the original owner, Burlington Mills. In the same way, the Roman Catholic Archdiocese of Austin, Texas, reportedly purchased a chain of 22 Massachusetts nursing homes for $4,700,000, then leased them back to the original owners, Geriatrics Management. The deal was said to call for payments to be completed in 15 years, entirely out of income from the nursing homes.

But perhaps no transaction was more ecumenical than a

two-stage one whose first step, in 1954, was the purchase by the Methodist-related Wesleyan University in Illinois of two California hotels: the Roosevelt in Hollywood and the El Rancho in Sacramento. The price was reported to be $10,000,000, of which only $200,000 was in cash, the remainder in a mortgage. Within five years Wesleyan had its $200,000 cash outlay back, plus tax-free profits for the period, and the hotels were resold to the St. Andrew Roman Catholic Church in Chicago.

Lease-backs are an "excellent hedge" against inflation, J. C. Cantrell, executive secretary of the Baptist Foundation of Texas, told a *Wall Street Journal* reporter. The foundation reported obtaining nearly 17 percent of its gross income of $2,800,000 in a recent year from lease-backs—ranging from supermarkets to service stations—though they comprised only 14 percent of its investments.

There may be questions about the ethics of such self-liquidating lease-back transactions—or "bootstrap purchases," as they are known in financial jargon—but there presently is no question about their legality. This was affirmed by the U.S. Supreme Court in the 1965 *Clay Brown* decision upholding special tax treatment for a bootstrap purchase of a sawmill and lumber business. At the same time, the Justices recommended that Congress reexamine policy in this area.

"In any realistic sense," according to one minority opinion, "the Government's grant of a tax exemption was used by the [exempt purchaser] as part of an arrangement that allowed it to buy a business that in fact cost it nothing. I cannot believe that Congress intended such a result. . . . Unless Congress repairs the damage done by the Court's holding, I should think that charities will soon own a considerable number of closed corporations, the owners of which will see no good reason to continue paying taxes at ordinary income rates. . . ."

A bill to plug the tax loophole which encourages boot-strap purchases was introduced in 1966 by House Ways and Means Committee Chairman Wilbur Mills, Democrat of Arkansas, and Congressman John W. Byrnes, Republican of Wisconsin, the committee's ranking minority member. At this writing, however, the churches have remained silent on the bill—as in 1950, refraining from publicly communicating either approval or disapproval to Congressmen—and Congress has failed to act on the measure.

III

In a capitalist economy, certainly, there is nothing sinister about the accumulation of wealth by individuals or by enterprises chartered for the purpose of making a profit. On the contrary, wealth lawfully amassed symbolizes to some degree the successful functioning of the profit system, for it is assumed that profits result only as consumer wants are satisfied with some efficiency in the marketplace. Likewise, the accumulation of property by nonprofit institutions may be not only legal but socially desirable, to the extent that such assets are obtained lawfully; are not in fact treated as gifts; and further the purpose for which the nonprofit institution was established.

Does the rapidly accumulating wealth of organized religion materially assist in the purpose for which it was granted tax-exempt status? On the contrary, in examining history, theologians and historians of highest repute seem to concur that it is precisely in periods when the church has been most successful materially that it has been least vigorous and influential.

Surely, despite their wealth and privileges, the churches today are scarcely in ascendancy, either in their social influence or in assuring a secure future. Church attendance has steadily declined: on an average Sunday only a minority—45 percent—of the nation's adults attend a worship service. Further, according to the 1968 *Yearbook of American Churches,* church membership enrollment has slipped to its slowest pace since before World War II, having fallen proportionately behind the rate of national population increase for the second consecutive year; for the first time in recent years, all of the nation's 12 major religious bodies—Protestant, Roman Catholic, Orthodox, and Jewish—experienced not only a relative decline in the number of young people enrolled in church and Sunday schools, but an actual numerical decline as well. The percentage of seminary students in the basic bachelor of divinity program leading to the ministry also has declined (though registration for advanced teaching careers did enable seminaries to report an over-all 4 percent increase in enrollment for 1967-68). And several major denominations reported decreased income.

Moreover, an estimated 70,000 congregations are without regular pastors; churches continue to be plagued by resignations from the parish ministry, especially in the under-forty age range; and emotional breakdowns among ministers are a growing problem. Some 10,000 Protestant ministers are receiving some form of psychiatric care, according to one report by the director of the Academy of Religion and Mental Health, and the United Presbyterian Church, among others, has signed a contract with the Menninger Clinic for diagnostic services to ministers. Gallup polls reveal that approximately half of today's Americans—including nearly two-thirds of its college students—believe that the churches are losing their influence on daily life.

"The ethically oriented Christian seems to be deterred rather than challenged by what he finds in church," Rodney Stark and Charles Y. Glock report in *American Piety: The Nature of Religious Commitment,* first volume in a three-part study for the University of California Press. "The more a man is committed to ethicalism the less likely he is to contribute funds or participate in the life of the church."

My own candid talks with churchmen in connection with several national magazine reports reinforce and in some measure validate these observations. In one instance ("Why I Quit the Ministry," *Saturday Evening Post,* Nov. 17, 1962), my assignment was to interview several dozen able ministers and ex-ministers and discuss, through the story of one of them, why—despite a postwar religious "revival"—the ministry has such severe recruiting and dropout problems.

A minister, like a denominational organization, I was told, operates on two levels: the prophetic, or teaching and counseling level; and the corporate, or administrative level. Tension between these levels is unending. And today, despite rumblings of reform and sporadic social involvement by a courageous minority, the corporate and administrative aspects of the ministry and denominational organizations predominate.

"In the typical parish," as one ex-minister explained, "the minister is not the permanent fixture; the congregation is. Like a human organism, its first rule is survival, and beyond that, security. There must be a building in which to meet; staff; inputs of new members, preferably congenial and well-heeled people; and provision for future needs. A minister may try to fight The System—and a number of good ones do—but his success and career survival are measured on the corporate level by the degree to which he can help meet these parish goals.

"This means that he is always under pressure to increase the membership: Numbers signify success. He also is expected to build or renovate: Building signifies progress. This requires funds. It also consumes enormous energy. The supervisory time and energy of the minister must come at the expense of other goals. This heightens the tension between the prophetic and corporate imperatives of the ministry, and it becomes almost impossible to keep the corporate aspect from increasingly impinging on the prophetic side."

Indeed, the "comfort reflex" and "edifice complex" are so pervasive that, Vice President Hubert Humphrey reminded the General Assembly of the National Council of Churches in a speech, the Protestant and Orthodox churches of the nation spend only about $500 million a year on services to those outside the churches—"only 41 cents a month for everyone who belongs to a church in America." Of the $75,000,000 received by the Protestant churches in Chicago in a typical recent year, according to the best available estimate, "less than $6,000,000 was spent outside the local congregations where the money was raised."

So firmly is this tendency toward home-parish aggrandizement embedded in local congregations that most ministers are in the doleful position of the rector of a large suburban church which received a $300,000 bequest. The bequest requires that the estate's executors, rather than the church's vestrymen, determine how the money should be spent—a restriction which, the minister confided to friends, caused him privately to rejoice.

"Now we can actually fill an urgent need—establish a counseling center," he said. "If the decision rested with the vestrymen we'd probably end up with a larger parking lot or God knows what other elaborate adornment."

Nor are economic pressures any less ruthless on denominational hierarchies. With Parkinsonian inevitability, economic expansion and membership increments bring proliferating levels of authority. (According to one survey, only 59.1 percent of the Protestant Episcopal clergy in this country are in charge of congregations.) Parkinsonian forces also tend to dominate over-all budgeting. The Reverend John R. Fry, min-

ister of the First Presbyterian Church in Chicago, was in a
unique position to observe this while serving as news editor
of the magazine *Presbyterian Life,* at the headquarters of the
Presbyterian Church in the U.S.A.

"Most of the money allocated to boards and agencies
pays for the salaries of staff, real estate, upkeep, and program
materials," he says. "[If cut in budget] a board must then
fire staff, or reduce salaries; it must jeopardize real estate
holdings. . . . The presenters [to the General Assembly] do
not mention that the cash outlay for administrative and allied
costs represents an estimated 70 per cent of the total amount
of money designated in the budget as a general mission item.
. . . The denomination seems to want to delude itself. The
officials and its membership . . . share the fantasy that they
are not an ecclesiastical business juggernaut."

All these forces place unrelenting economic stress on
individual parishes and denominational structures. Consequently, today whenever one moves from one community to
another and joins a church, he is apt to discover: (1) the
church is in the midst of a major capital fund drive; (2) it has
just completed one; or (3) it is about to embark on one. And
this drive is likely to be for the purpose of: (1) building an
entirely "new, modern, and adequate church plant" at a recently acquired site; (2) extensively renovating the existing
plant, including perhaps a new organ, central air condition-
ing, new youth rooms, a chapel, and sizable off-street parking
facilities; or (3) raising the money needed to complete such
projects which were begun earlier on a stage-by-stage basis
whose "last stage" now has arrived.

In addition to capital fund drives, of course, there are
regular campaigns to meet the church's annual budget, plus
drives to assist in the capital needs of the parent denomination and nearby denominational hospitals or colleges. In
short, whatever parish one joins, the major ongoing congrega-

tional activity probably will be fund-raising—much of it for building or administrative expense of some sort.

Because a sizable or growing church plant requires not only money but management, one also will find the parish governing board (by whatever name it is known) heavily peopled with representatives of the town's business and professional community—ideally, perhaps, a banker; a lawyer; a doctor or dentist; a real estate man; and a corporation executive or two. In less prestigious parishes, though the community status of board members is less imposing, the principle remains the same: enlist a heavy representation of members who have attained the greatest career success and, therefore, have acquired pragmatic judgment and experience. Most will be major contributors to the parish budget; most will be middle-aged men; almost all will be property owners; all probably will be members of at least one business or professional organization in the community (or perhaps a trade union); and, except in the newest suburbs, several will have local roots extending back several generations.

Such elite members are, alas, in relatively short supply. As a result, the young ex-minister who became the subject of the *Post* article told me, one sometimes finds ministers of the larger churches in a community stalking them as rigorously as football coaches trying to recruit all-star tackles. "One minister," he recalls, "even went so far as to proselyte a wealthy family from another minister's church."

Wherever one moves, he will find, too, that the role of the minister is fairly standardized. If it is a Protestant church, the minister and his family will live in a parish-owned parsonage, and his tenure will in effect be at the sufferance of the aforementioned parish Establishment (though in some denominations assignments are formally apportioned at a higher level, and in all of them the approval of one's peers as well as his hierarchical superiors is important). In such denominations as the Methodist and Roman Catholic Churches, of course, advancement can be obtained only through parish appointments bestowed by one's superiors.

If a parish is a small, inner-city, or rural one, it probably will have a very young minister (perhaps one under thirty, or even a seminary student), or one nearing or past retirement age. If middle-sized or large, the parish will have a minister who is past thirty-five, perhaps forty—plus one or more assistants. Regardless of age, the minister probably will have had no other vocational experience outside his profession, nor will he have appreciable financial reserves—if any. The median ministerial salary in this country in 1967, according to the National Council of Churches, was slightly less than $7,000 a year. Roman Catholic priests, however, may receive as little as $100 a month (the average in New York City recently was reported as $225 monthly for parish priests; $150 to $175 for their parish assistants). The whole appointment and compensation pattern of parish ministers—Protestant and Catholic—in short, will tend to reinforce orientation toward the organization.

One will find two principal ways in which the minister can unfailingly attract his superiors' attention: (1) preside over a conspicuous gain or loss in members and parish income, or a major failure or success in a building program; or (2) become involved in a congregational imbroglio, perhaps due to "radical" theological statements or involvement in social causes outside the church—especially civil rights or pacifism.

If the minister comes to the attention of superiors in a favorable way—i.e., through a conspicuous membership gain or building program, he at once will become the talk of various ministerial and lay conferences and be promptly tabbed for promotion (e.g., to a church with a larger membership and plant than his present one). If he gets into "trouble" (e.g., presides over a membership or income decline or becomes a subject of controversy within his congregation), he will be admonished by his superiors, in all good faith, to measure his situation carefully so as not to jeopardize his own or his parish's future; and, if his relations with his congregational Establishment appear irreconcilable, he will be transferred and probably in effect demoted. If not demoted, he will be assigned to a "special situation" in which an unconventional congregation—perhaps in the inner-city—seeks a theological progressive or social activist as minister; or he temporarily will leave the parish ministry for teaching or a social-action committee or agency of his denomination, or perhaps an interfaith group.

Who are the principal instigators of such "demotions"? Invariably, be the parish Protestant or be it Catholic, the responsibility falls to the same group of organization-minded laymen who have been entrusted with congregational leadership because of their business or administrative know-how and their community status. Few but the most dynamic and persuasive ministers succeed in operating counter to these individuals' basic wishes for long, for their participation in the management and financial support of congregational affairs and church expansion programs has come to be regarded as imperative, and their power is great.

Sometimes this power is wielded openly. In Washington, D.C., for instance, a teen-agers' music festival at which miniskirted dancers were photographed in Washington Cathedral was said by its dean, the Very Reverend Francis B. Sayre, Jr., to have cost $500,000 in prospective contributions. And in the affluent Chicago suburb of Oak Park, Illinois, the aggressiveness of an associate pastor of the 1,500-member First Presbyterian Church in local human rights and antiwar protests resulted in a decline in contributions to the church and, in December 1967, announcement by the associate that he

was being released from the staff to "appease" parish op-
ponents who had applied "economic pressure."

Most often, though, this power is wielded silently and
cautiously behind closed doors of a church, the cumulative
effect being more decisive than any single incident. The
young ex-minister with whom I collaborated on the *Post* article confirmed this at his suburban Protestant parish when,
after limited opposition to some ideas, he encountered massive resistance to two seemingly innocuous reforms.

One measure was directed at making "membership in
the church more meaningful" than heretofore. "It long had
troubled me that we listed 800 members and only half ever
came to church even periodically," he said. "At least 100
'members' no longer even lived in the suburb. Why should we
continue to carry this deadwood? It cluttered up the rolls,
demeaned the image of the church, deceived the inactives
into thinking that they had a religion of which the church
approved, and heightened the impression that ours was an
'anything goes' organization."

Accordingly, he reminded the church Session of its responsibility for "membership discipline" and suggested,
"Let's begin enforcing this, at least with minimum requirements that members attend worship frequently and consis-
tently support the church financially." "We'll think about it,"
the banker who headed the Session told him.

"But," added the ex-minister, " 'thinking' is as far as it
got—Session members, many of whom had business relationships with the 'respectable' inactives, were afraid to move."

Not long afterward, in an endeavor to separate the
church from participation in funeral customs which he regarded as pagan and overcommercialized, he "preached a
strongly worded sermon on the Christian view of death . . .
wrote a pamphlet about the subject, with reasons why an
expensive casket and more than a simple display of flowers

are questionable as Christian tributes ... announced the establishment of a memorial fund for contributions which could tastefully honor deceased church members." Though he had discussed his position in advance with a funeral director and two florists who were church officers, he recalled, "after the service all three howled as if they were in pain."

"You're picking on our business!" said a florist.

"Funeral costs are none of your business," complained the undertaker.

"If such things aren't the church's affair, then what is?" the minister asked.

"Still," he told me, "they were adamant in their opposition to my action, so much so that they began phoning other prominent members. ... As usual, a serious-minded minority in the congregation was with me. But the power structure of the congregation placed pressure on the banker who dominated the Session. ... 'You had better go slow on this,' he told me. 'We like you. But if you get too controversial we'll have to ask you to leave.' "

The minister, after contemplating this and other experiences, finally decided, "This was not the ministry to which I had felt a call. Nor did there appear to be any hope that things would change for the better in my lifetime. My life would be wasted as a recreation director for what essentially seemed to me to be little more than a USO for civilians or a Sunday morning mutual admiration society. ... The majority of today's church members refuse to care. In this refusal, most remaining members and much of their chosen church hierarchy blandly acquiesce. How, then, can a minister rationalize devoting his life to the organization which results, a superficial extension of society? How can he live with himself if he does?"

The young man, after resigning from the ministry, returned to college to qualify as a university instructor and, eventually, a career in public service—some vocation, as he put it, "in the mainstream of life."

His former parish, meanwhile, like that of others which have undergone similar experiences, remains relatively unchanged, except for the absence of several former members who left in despair over the same circumstances which occasioned his leaving. The parish plant remains handsome and well maintained. The parish membership continues to reflect the socioeconomic profile and the general attitudes of its constituent community. And the town itself—a well-manicured, conventionally Anglo-Saxon suburb with typical problems of genteel racism, divorce, alcoholism, and youthful nihilism—outwardly, at least, also appears the same.

"Almost," as one resident put it, "as if that young man with his new ideas had never come in and impatiently started to push the congregation in a direction everyone could see it didn't want to go."

IV

Under United States law, a religious body not only is a private membership organization; it also enjoys specific Constitutional immunity from outside interference. This basic freedom, however, does not mean that materialism in organized religion is beyond the legitimate concern of society. Indeed, for various reasons, such tendencies make public policy affecting the church a prime candidate for social scrutiny.

Not the least of these reasons is the dilution of moral leadership inherent in such materialism. In almost every discussion of the Constitutional rationale for church tax exemptions, the "constructive function" of organized religion in society is prominently mentioned. In the 1964 report of the National Study Conference on Church and State, which was sponsored by the General Board of the National Council of Churches of Christ in the U.S.A., for example [see appendix], religious institutions' "useful functions in society" were given as one of two grounds for the soundness of "certain forms" of tax exemptions. "Without such institutions performing these functions," the report declared, "any society, particularly one with democratic objectives, might be seriously crippled." If, as the troubled ex-minister who quit his pulpit wrote in the *Post,* the church becomes "little more than a USO for civilians or a Sunday morning mutual admiration society," the human family is indeed crippled—possibly critically, if the result is that grave problems such as war, racism, poverty, overpopulation, crime, and family instability overwhelm us.

This paradox—that, as man's survival depends more and more on moral direction, the institution on which he has depended for that direction grows more impotent—surely is one of the tragedies of our time. For, notwithstanding the bold example of an innovative minority of leading Christian thinkers, organized religion for the past quarter-century, at least, has assumed not the role of society's moral leader but of a follower. Science's stripping away of ignorance, superstition, and mythology has provided an authoritative new base for exploration of man's classic questions of the soul: Who am I; where did I come from; why am I here? Secular scholars have constructed the beginnings of social sciences which, for all their imperfections and immaturity, have demonstrated their capacity to help man systematically understand and modify the behavior of individuals, societies, and social institutions. Government and secular agencies—building on one of Christianity's noblest traditions—have become the dominant vehicles of ministering to the poor, the ignorant, the ill, the oppressed. Segregated, insulated, narcissistic, rich, the average American denominational institution, like other vast institutions in society, has come to seem both impersonal and impervious to individual influence, breeding a feeling of anomie compounded of superficiality and frustration.

"It is," the editors of *World Outlook,* a leading Methodist journal, observed in a recent editorial, "the feeling that the church is a machine, not a community, and that the machine is running us, not we the machine. Too much organization, too much program, too much direction from the top —these are familiar complaints that are repeated over and over again."

In addition to stunting the churches' leadership potential, religious materialism exacts a stupendous price in diver-
sion of economic resources to essentially narrow, unconstruc-
tive social purposes. Aid for the poor, ill, and uneducated
always is in scant supply. Particularly in a period of cataclys-
mic change such as now and the immediate future, the diver-
sion of the limited resources realistically available for social
purposes can be devastating. As John W. Gardner warned in a
speech shortly before retiring as U.S. Secretary of Health,
Education, and Welfare: "[Man's] increasing confidence, justified or not, that he can take a hand in determining his own
fate and can rid himself of at least a few of the ancient
afflictions . . . places a very heavy burden on man and his
institutions."

But perhaps the least complicated, most pragmatically
compelling reason for the scrutiny of organized religion's eco-
nomics is a growing tax squeeze—at all governmental levels—
which appears to have set government and a variety of exempt institutions on a collision course. Three decades ago,
only about 12 percent of the real property in the United
States was tax-exempt. Today, the figure has risen to 30 percent, with valuations of more than $325 billion—according to
one authority, "more than the combined total real estate in
the twenty largest cities in the United States." Nationally, according to Martin A. Larson in *Church Wealth and Business
Income,* assuming an average property tax of 50 mills of
assessed valuation and 20 mills of true valuation, "all exempt
property . . . is now escaping an annual tax levy of $7 billion,
which averages about $140 for every family; the private-
exempt is escaping $2.7 billion, or $54 for each family; religious organizations alone are avoiding levies of $1.6 billion,
or $32 for every family in the nation."

In one state—Minnesota—the Minneapolis *Star* reported
the valuation of tax-exempt real estate to be growing twice as
fast as that of taxable property, with one-fifth of the state's

total real-property valuation, as of 1962, under tax "shelters." In a number of cities, the "free list" constitutes an
even higher proportion of the real-property rolls. In 1960, for
example, a Southern Baptist Study Paper noted that 37.5
percent of the real property in Boston and 35.9 percent of
that in Nashville was tax-exempt. In New York, the ratio is
about one-third, and in Philadelphia the figure is 40 percent.

The revenue plight of Dubuque, Iowa, a scenic community of 60,000 persons in the wooded palisades of the
upper Mississippi River valley, is particularly instructive. The
Metropolitan Planning Commission, after an area study, estimated that more than 40 percent of the city's 62,000 acres
of developed land—or $1 for every $3 worth of taxable property—is tax-exempt. The exempt buildings, an Associated
Press report noted, include seminaries, colleges, church
homes, and more than 40 churches with related buildings.

"Two-thirds of the children attend parochial schools,"
the reporter stated. "There are three church-affiliated colleges—the University of Dubuque, which is Presbyterian and
coeducational; Clarke College, Catholic, for women, and
Loras College, Catholic, for men. There are also Wartburg
Seminary, Lutheran; six Catholic convents, two major Catholic hospitals, the Catholic archdiocesan offices, and the archbishop's manse. More church building is in progress."

Local taxes have been increased with regularity, in part
due to three consecutive years of flooding of the downtown
by the Mississippi River, but viewing the 1968 municipal
budget, Dubuque's city manager foresaw a $275,000 deficit.
Should local taxes be raised? "The rate already is crowding
the legal limit," the reporter pointed out. Should the city
borrow? "There are both legal and practical ceilings on
debt," he cautioned. Might payment of some taxes on church
properties help? Obviously, said the city manager—but, aware
of the delicacy of the issues, he was unwilling to state un-
equivocally that this should be done.

"The dilemma of Dubuque," the report concluded, "is repeated in thousands of towns and counties across the country."

Property of various governmental echelons—parks, post offices, military posts, city halls, schools—in general comprises the largest single tax-exempt bloc. Next come properties owned by churches and religious organizations: Catholic, $44.5 billion; Protestant, $28 billion; and Jewish, $7 billion, according to projections in *Church Wealth and Business Income* based on representative local samplings. Despite nonpayment of taxes, all must be provided with certain community services—police, fire, sanitation, and street maintenance, for instance. In communities where one-fifth to one-third of local property valuation is tax-exempt—no longer uncommon—the burden on the local revenue structure is obvious.

"The problem is serious," says Paul V. Corusy, executive director of the International Association of Assessing Officers. "The property tax base is being eroded."

State and local officials, who live even closer than Congressmen to their constituencies, for the most part have been more leery than national legislators of treading on churchly toes. But a few states and communities have demonstrated at least tentative initiative in this touchy area. Tennessee, for one, now limits churches to one tax-free parsonage for each congregation; Kentucky's Attorney General has ruled that church-owned buses are subject to the same property taxes as privately owned vehicles, and that property purchased for future expansion is not exempt from real-estate taxes; the legislatures of several states have investigated the idea of authorizing a levy against churches at least for essential community services.

In Oregon, in fact, bills were introduced in the legislature in 1963 and 1965 to tax church properties at one-third of their assessed valuations to pay for fire, police, sanitation, and other essential services. Neither bill passed, but when the issue was raised again in last year's session, though the Oregon Council of Churches opposed it, the influential Greater Portland Council of Churches supported it, and it seems certain to be introduced again.

In Harrisburg, Pennsylvania, about a dozen church properties, most of them used as parking lots, have been returned to real-estate tax rolls on recommendations of a special task force; Baltimore has persuaded church-owned housing developments to pay taxes equal to one-fourth of those on privately owned apartments; nearly a dozen communities in Colorado collect "partial taxes" from churches for municipal services; and dozens of cities—including Milwaukee, Wisconsin; Anchorage, Alaska; and West Palm Beach, Florida—have disallowed previously unquestioned exemptions for properties not used directly for religious purposes.

At the federal level, the Internal Revenue Service also has announced its intention to require nonprofit groups to pay federal taxes on magazine advertising revenues. Affected by the announcement, among others, are the advertising-fat *National Geographic* and the *Journal of the American Medical Association*. But the proposal—which several nonprofit organizations promptly pledged to contest in court—could also apply to the unrelated business income of religious publications.

Perhaps most significantly at the federal level, Assistant Secretary of the Treasury Stanley S. Surrey in 1966 asked Congress to eliminate tax exemptions on "bootstrap purchases" by nonprofit organizations—including religious and related institutions. In doing so, he released a statement of more than transitory significance for its brevity and clarity in reviewing perplexing economic and political questions inherent in this controversial concession. Surrey's case, in part, against the viability of this exemption as sound policy for either the public or the churches:

"First, in any acquisition in which the purchase price is to be financed from the future earnings of the transferred property, tax-exempt organizations are peculiarly suited to pay a substantially higher price—and pay it more rapidly—than a taxable purchaser could afford. They can, in effect, make available to the seller the additional business earnings which would have been paid to the Government as taxes had the purchaser been taxable. . . . With the dual attractions to sellers of high prices and Supreme Court-approved capital gains treatment, it seems quite likely that, unless something is done, a substantial unplanned shift of productive property to the exempt sector of our economy will occur. . . .

"A second undesirable result typically attends borrowing by exempt organizations for investment purposes. The price inflation characteristic of *Brown*-type transactions . . . deflects, to the personal benefit of private parties, a substantial portion of the advantage which Congress intended tax exemption to produce for the organizations upon which it conferred the exemption. . . .

"A third unfortunate consequence follows from exempt-organization investment borrowing. This investment borrowing enables an exempt organization to convert its tax exemption into a self-sufficient device for the production of capital. . . . the organization which makes such use of its exemption can sever itself from reliance upon contributors or members and eliminate the healthful scrutiny of its purposes and activities which that reliance implies. By this extension of its exemption privilege to borrowed assets and this separation from dependence upon contributors or members, the organization begins a multiplication of its holdings which bears no relation to the community's evaluation of its exempt activities; it embarks upon an extension of its economic holdings which is limited only by the financial acumen and commercial skills of its managers. . . .

"Let me emphasize that the present fortuitous, but very powerful, incentive for the transfer of businesses and other classes of productive property to exempt organizations requires effective and prompt Congressional action. . . . If Congress does not deal with the problem—and deal with it quickly—a great many more [transfers of businesses and other classes of productive property to exempt organizations] will take place."

If Congress does not act, might the courts intervene?

The Supreme Court's *Clay Brown* opinion indicates that its first preference, at least as to regulation of bootstrap purchases, is for Congressional action. Nor is there any present indication that the justices see a "substantial federal question" in general church property tax exemptions. When the Maryland Court of Appeals in 1966 ruled against militant atheist Madelyn Murray in a lawsuit challenging real estate tax exemptions for churches and synagogues, for example, the Supreme Court declined to review the decision. And previously, in *Schempp-Murray,* Justice Brennan specified: "Nothing we hold today questions the propriety of certain tax deductions or exemptions which incidentally benefit churches and religious institutions, along with many secular charities and nonprofit organizations."

At the same time, several lower courts have taken judicial notice of changing relationships which could lead to reinterpretation of *laissez-faire* exemption policies. The Supreme Court of Tennessee, in delineating certain property tax exemptions in *Baptist Sunday School Board vs. City of Nashville,* for instance, stated:

> It is a matter of current history, which the Court judicially knows, that during the last quarter of a century, the tax burdens of the individual taxpayer have grown increasingly heavier. The care and support of the poor

and needy, formerly the work of charities, has been largely taken over by
government, federal, state, and municipal, and is carried on by means of
public taxation, and our cities are constantly struggling to find new sources
of revenue to meet the growing needs for police and fire protection,
schools and social welfare.

The policy of tax exemption of religious institutions, established
when they were struggling to get along, has enabled them, during the last
quarter of a century, to acquire large real estate holdings and to accumu-
late great wealth; and many of them are engaged in operating various kinds
of secular businesses tax-free, in competition with other like businesses
that are taxed. This development creates inequities and endangers both the
churches and the state.

The Supreme Court, too, in several revealing declarations, has indicated that the over-all effect of religious tax
exemptions, not merely their history of tacit approval over
the years, could be a basis of later redefinition of their propriety under the First Amendment prohibition of state "establishment" of religion. As Justice Clark stated in *Schempp-
Murray:*

> The test [of laws challenged under the Establishment Clause] may
> be stated as follows: What are the purpose and the primary effect of the
> enactment? If either is the advancement or inhibition of religion then the
> enactment exceeds the scope of legislative power as circumscribed by the
> Constitution. That is to say that to withstand the strictures of the estab-
> lishment clause there must be a secular legislative purpose and a primary
> effect that neither advances nor inhibits religion.

"To date," says attorney Andrew D. Tanner in *The
Question of Tax Exemption for Churches,* "the Court's decisions do not *preclude* the removal of tax exemptions, but it
seems unlikely the Court will decide this question unless and
until 1) 'tax exemptions' are interpreted as being the same as
'appropriating money to finance religion'; 2) tax exemptions
given other types of charitable organizations are removed;
and 3) economic necessity forces it to be done."

V

Where do churchmen stand on the issues of church acquisitiveness, business interests, and blanket immunity from
taxation?

As has been suggested, there is a vast range of views—
from those who see in present trends the ingredients of a
fatal poison, to those who admit nothing inappropriate in
church-owned contracting, food-chain, or bra and girdle
firms. Among those who profess distress over the current
situation, there also is, as one might suspect, considerably
more talk than action. But the outlines of a movement away
from the status quo are visible, if only among an embattled,
persevering, somewhat young minority.

Perhaps the most vigorous orientation toward change
has occurred in the Roman Catholic Church—much of it stim-
ulated by such Vatican II declarations as that of Cardinal
Giacomo Lercaro: that the church's imperative requirement
is "holy poverty"; "a definition of the ways in which the
material resources of the Church may be used . . . in accor-
dance with the words: 'Gold and silver have I none, but what
I have I give you.'" This spirit, for example, has moved a
group of Chicago priests to openly challenge Cardinal John P.
Cody's ten-year, $250-million building program as "placing

too much emphasis on organizational structure and outdated forms of the church." The church, they warned, "may well be harnessed by an overstructured development and thereby endanger its present and future mobility."

In Woodstock, Maryland, not long ago, eleven Jesuit seminarians and a Georgetown University faculty priest publicly questioned whether the Society of Jesus is conforming to Christian values in providing $800,000 for further construction on the Shrine of the Immaculate Conception in Washington, D.C. And in Richardson, Texas, according to a report in *Ave Maria,* the national Catholic weekly, parishioners of St. Paul the Apostle Church "still have no satisfactory answers to why the Paulist priests, who have served their parish so successfully in the last eleven years, were suddenly asked to leave the diocese" because of "lack of independent financial support" at the same time the diocesan leadership "has been funneling millions of dollars into the diocesan-run University of Dallas and a new plush Holy Trinity Seminary which includes a heated swimming pool, stereo room, a carpeted dining room, and private suites for administrators."

But perhaps the most celebrated American Catholic church-construction imbroglio occurred in San Francisco following a 1962 fire that destroyed the huge Gothic St. Mary's Cathedral. After the fire, the San Francisco diocese at once purchased a new site and began a $15,500,000 building fund drive, which within a short time netted $13,500,000. Included in the building plans were a new $6,000,000 cathedral, a seminary, a home for the aged, and three new high schools. A local chapter of the Catholic Interracial Council asked that $1,000,000 of the solicitations be allocated to help Bay area poor, but the request was denied. A few months later CIC members petitioned for a complete halt to the cathedral project until low-cost housing for the poor and other community social needs had been served. Again the petitioners were rejected—and, after Mid-Peninsula CIC members picketed the 1965 diocesan ordination ceremonies, they were informed that a $1,000-a-year diocesan contribution for scholarships to minority youths would not be renewed.

Episcopal Bishop C. Kilmer Myers of California offered the area's Catholics the joint use of Grace Episcopal Cathedral, but Archbishop Joseph T. McCracken declined, maintaining that the scheduling of "six or seven masses" on Sunday besides Episcopal services made such sharing impossible. When excavation work began in 1967, 27 local priests declared in an "Open Letter to the Catholics of the United States": "We deeply regret our common mistakes here in San Francisco. We hope other Christians—even on the parish level —will learn from our failures." And a group of Catholic laymen petitioned for a halt in construction, a reevaluation of "the Christian priorities of the human needs in San Francisco," and an accounting of expenditures on the cathedral to date. In a press statement they asked:

"Has the church committed itself to constructing a Golden Calf on the land where over 500 family units were rented for an average of less than $55 a month; where over 50 per cent of the people were of minority groups; and where 30 per cent were dependent on welfare assistance?"

Construction of the cathedral has gone forward nonetheless, and CIC members have turned their attention to requiring the builders and their unions to guarantee equal opportunities to nonwhites seeking employment on the project.

The Most Reverend Fulton J. Sheen, shortly after becoming Bishop of Rochester, New York, declared: "There never should be a new church built here that costs more than, say, $1,000,000. If a diocese insists on spending more for a church, it ought to pay something like a 20 per cent tax for missions." Later he imposed such a tax "on all construction and reconstruction in the diocese . . . graduated according to the expenditure, [to] be given to the poor in this city and diocese and to the poor of the world."

New York Episcopal Bishop Horace W. B. Donegan's pre-Christmas 1967 announcement of a halt to construction on the Cathedral of St. John the Divine in Manhattan was comparably dramatic. Of some $12,000,000 still needed for completion, $2,000,000 had been pledged in six months; but, said the Bishop, "the whole urban crisis" had raised a question about such endeavors. "There will," he said, "be no fund-raising drive for its completion . . . until there is greater evidence that the anguish and despair of our unadvantaged people has been relieved."

Episcopalians also have sharply questioned the spending of more money on the towering Washington, D.C., Cathedral, which has cost $30,000,000 to date and will require at least $20,000,000 more to complete. Indeed, spokesmen for several faiths have proposed a moratorium on all new-church construction—for a year, two, even five years.

"Perhaps," Ave Maria editorialized, "that is the best suggestion of all. It would not only cause us to 'make do' with what we have; it would give us time to re-examine our purposes, our direction, and our means. . . . Let us keep the great churches as monuments, nostalgic and uplifting. But let us build no more. The glory of God in our age is the men who care about their fellow men."

Because church wealth could not be liquidated overnight, even were there a wave of resolve to do so, increasing attention also is being paid to the end use of church savings and investment funds in commercial institutions. For money is power—albeit secular power which can become an end in itself—and power is never neutral. Does a bank, by its credit decisions, help undergird a foreign government which enforces racist policies? The Methodist Board of Missions decided that the giant First National City Bank of New York did precisely this in remaining in a consortium which offers revolving credit to South Africa, and in February 1968 the board announced an intention to transfer a $10,000,000 investment portfolio from the bank as a "tangible, symbolic protest."

"It is a moral obligation of the churches to throw whatever light they can upon the dark wounds of suffering in our world," said Mrs. Porter Brown, general secretary of the board. "Surely it is our obligation to bring to bear what conscience we can upon the plight of the colored people who suffer under apartheid."

Does a great corporation, by its recruitment policies and the actions of certain executives, help rigidify a community power structure hostile to militant neighborhood federations seeking to organize the poor? In Rochester, New York, a nucleus of ministers and laymen supporting a community-action movement named FIGHT decided this was the case with the Eastman Kodak Company; they bought single shares of stock to gain admission to the firm's stockholder meeting and help publicize eventually successful efforts to obtain the company's cooperation in recruitment and training of jobless residents.

Do companies with which churches regularly deal practice racial discrimination in employment and promotion? Protestants, Jews, and Catholics active in Project Equality, initiated by the National Catholic Conference for Interracial Justice, document such cases and are persuading several dozen parishes and dioceses to bring pressure on such companies to change.

"Those who say the church should not use power in society are naïve," says Mathew Ahmann, executive director of the National Catholic Conference for Interracial Justice. "The church uses power every day and should use it carefully for a variety of social objectives."

There also has been increasingly searching questioning of shibboleths about the present structure of church tax exemptions. Indeed, several authorities have reached the seemingly heretical conclusion that not only might some exemptions be modified without destroying the church, but all could be withdrawn without fatal effects.

A report of a National Council of Churches Study Committee on Tax Exemption for Churches, for instance, listed as one of its "guiding principles": "For itself the church asks of government no more than freedom. ... In the final analysis ... the question of whether churches are granted ... tax exemptions is peripheral to the church's ability to function and to carry out its mission. ...."

There is, as yet, no substantial support for terminating the basic tax exemption on property used for worship and other directly religious purposes. But a National Council of Churches study in 1965-66 found notable sentiment for taxing churches' business activities, and prominent Protestant groups have issued policy statements to this effect [see appendix]. One is the Southern Baptist Study Paper adopted in 1960 which says: "... Federal income tax exemption [on unrelated business income] tends to 1) encourage promotion of or participation in secular business to the detriment of the principal mission of the church; 2) encourage morally unjustifiable arrangements with businessmen or companies to reduce their income taxes; 3) discourage financial support of church activities by voluntary contributions of all members."

In 1958, the General Assembly of the United Presbyterian Church in the U.S.A. requested its denominational foundation "to make no investment in unrelated business where such income tax exemptions are allowable." In 1963 it further recommended that "congregations be encouraged to take the initiative in making contributions to local communities, in lieu of taxes, in recognition of police, fire, and other services provided by the government. ...."

A Methodist Study Commission on Church-Government Relations reported to the 1968 Methodist General Confer-

ence [see appendix]: "We do not perceive any justification
for government policies . . . which accord special privileges to
or provide differential treatment of churches in the matter of
exemption from tax liability. It is our conviction that the
special treatment accorded to 'churches and conventions or
associations of churches' with respect to exclusion of their
unrelated business income . . . ought to be discontinued."

The American Lutheran Church, in a "statement of policy and conviction" approved by its General Convention in
1966 [see appendix] declared: "Churches owning properties
and conducting business not exclusively and solely essential
to their religious, charitable, or educational ministry ought to
be subject to tax laws and policies equally applicable to those
governing profit-seeking individuals, partnerships, and corporations." Another statement, condemning church participation in activities unrelated to religious purposes, warned:
"Such commercialism, we believe, interferes with and con-
fuses the true task of the church . . . weakens and impover-
ishes the spiritual life of the church . . . exploits church membership for pecuniary advantage, and . . . damages the non-
members' picture of the church."

The Guild of St. Ives, a prestigious New York organization of Episcopal clergy and laymen, in a 1967 report on the
churches and taxation [see appendix] endorsed the levying
of income taxes, at a progressive rate over at least five years,
on the churches' real property and securities, and said of
unrelated businesses owned by religious organizations: "Such
unrelated businesses are operated in actual or potential competition with secular businesses and should, we feel, be accorded similar tax treatment."

And the National Association of Evangelicals charges
that profit-making by churches and their related organizations constitutes an unlawful subsidy forbidden by the First
Amendment.

Leading religious publications also advocate tax reform.

Says the Jesuit magazine *America*: "On the face of it, no exempt organization should be allowed to operate an unrelated business tax-free." *Catholic World* cautions: "If churches enjoy the same tax exemption on secular activities as other private agencies, they must also be prepared to forsake special exemptions when they engage in business activities unrelated to their religions or eleemosynary mission." And *Ave Maria* warns: "If a business is not related to the spiritual, charitable purpose of the church; if the tax exemption amounts to an unfair competitive business advantage; if the 'donation' to the church isn't really a donation at all, but only a way in which the donor can preserve or improve his financial situation—if these conditions are present, then the ecclesiastical administrators should be concerned about a scandal and about responsibilities to the nation."

The *Christian Science Monitor* terms modification of the exemption on unrelated business income imperative "to prevent American taxpayers from having in effect to subsidize religious forays into the competitive marketplace." *Christianity Today* points out that because "open-end opportunity for ecclesiastical involvement in untaxed business activities" tends to "entangle the church in economic administration to the detriment of her principal task" and "invites morally unjustifiable arrangements for financial advantage to churches . . . the time is propitious for sweeping study of the principle on which taxation and tax exemption rest." And *The Christian Century,* noting that "the power of the gospel does not depend on an accumulation of wealth," states: "Clergymen should see that they lobby for the common good and not for particular ecclesiastical favor."

There also appears to be burgeoning sentiment for some payment by churches for certain local-governmental services now being bestowed free. The American Lutheran Church, for example, has endorsed as "consistent with sound public policy" the levying upon churches of "nondiscriminatory charges for municipal services such as water, sewage, police, and fire protection [see appendix]." The Lutherans further state: "We believe that the churches should be willing to accept equitable taxation of parsonages and other dwellings ... in which their staff members reside."

The Methodist Study Commission on Church-Government Relations [see appendix] declares: "It is incumbent upon churches to consider ... responsibility to make appropriate contribution, in lieu of taxes, for essential services provided by government."

And a report adopted by the General Assembly of the United Presbyterian Church in the U.S.A. [see appendix] declares: "Congregations [should] be encouraged to take the initiative in making contributions to local communities, in lieu of taxes, in recognition of police, fire, and other services provided by local government. ... Those congregations which thus make voluntary contributions in lieu of taxes should not expect consideration or special favor in return. ..."

In Oregon, a position paper of the state's Council of Churches, while advocating retention of "the tax-exempt status of religious worship and education facilities," asked that "any abuses of laws pertaining to church-owned property tax exemptions be eliminated, including parsonages, manses, and residences for housing religious personnel; property which produces income from business operations, rentals or other activities; real estate held for future use or speculation." The Greater Portland Council of Churches concurred, adding: "We suggest that the legislature devise a system whereby the churches can be charged on a fee basis outside of tax assessment procedures for payment of such services."

"Neither churches nor charitable organizations expect to receive water from the city or gas or electricity from the utility companies without charge," said Robert K. Menzel, associate professor of religion at Concordia College, Portland, in a study paper for the Oregon Council. "Why should they expect equally important services at the expense of the community?"

A few nonprofit organizations already are volunteering payments to local governments in lieu of taxes. Near the end of 1967, the tax-exempt Twentieth Century Fund in New York City, in one of the most publicized such gestures, announced contribution of $10,000 to the city because, as an executive stated, "we are convinced that we have a civic responsibility to make some payment for the municipal services furnished to us." Several churches have adopted similar policies. In Cleveland, for example, the minister of the Unitarian Society asked his congregation to donate $10,000 to the city in lieu of taxes, and in Des Moines the Central Presbyterian Church voted to contribute up to $4,000 a year to city government—in addition to selling two parsonages and thenceforth paying its ministers monthly housing allowances.

Increasingly, too, support is mobilizing for requiring religious organizations to file public finâncial accountings, as now is the law in Canada. "All financial dealings of religious organizations should be made a matter of public record, unless a specific definite reason can be formulated for restricting information about a particular item," says the Reverend John L. Reedy, editor and publisher of *Ave Maria.* Indeed, according to Andrew D. Tanner in his study for the National Conference of Christians and Jews, a uniform law on tax exemption of church-related property should be formulated.

"Much confusion and conflict has been eliminated by adoption of uniform laws in other fields," he says. "A uniform law which has 'run the gauntlet' of study and scrutiny of religious leaders and denominations will have good chance for passage in the various states, and will influence tax exemption policies of the federal government. Such uniform law should provide:

"a) for listing, valuation, and reason for exemption of property on the tax rolls;

"b) for exemption of places of worship and necessary auxiliary land and buildings, property used for religious instruction and training, offices and facilities for administration of religious activities (including parking lots);

"c) that part of the property *not* used exclusively for church purposes, and which produces income from business rentals or other operations, *should* be taxed;

"d) church property held for *future use or speculation*, whether vacant or improved, should go on the tax roll, but be removed (without waiting for tax assessment date) as soon as used for church purposes;

"e) as to income taxes, tax liability should be determined by the source of income, rather than *use* to which the income is put.

"Joint conferences and studies armed with authentic compiled information above referred to," he adds, "should be conducted by and between leadership of the various denominations, to enable each denomination to determine policy to be followed with respect to tax exemptions. Adoption of some policy and action by several of the numerically stronger denominations will carry great weight with taxing authorities and other denominations. Certainly, study and frank discussion can contribute to the solution of the problem."

What might be the result if major tax reforms were adopted?

The consensus of reform-minded churchmen who have gone on record is that, in the long run, the churches could only benefit. Organized religion today is at one of its great transition points—perhaps a critical juncture that will deter-

mine whether a second Reformation is possible. Some scholars doubt that it is, if by "Reformation" is meant returning
Christian institutions to their earlier level of prominence. To
this school, it appears that Christian dogma has served its
historic function; man and society have transcended the
psychological, intellectual, and social developmental stages at
which the Christian church can command a central role in life
and society; this is a post-Christian era; hence, the church's
future role lies mainly in ceremonial functions (weddings,
christenings, funerals, etc.).

Thinkers of the opposite school—that Christianity is, indeed, timeless and infinitely self-renewing—are divided as to
the precise direction of a new Reformation. But, most agree,
greater wealth—more property, more privilege, more materialism—can never be the instrument of the churches' salvation.
On the contrary, church wealth, particularly when rooted in
pyramiding commercial entrepreneurship, represents an invi-
tation to almost inevitable oblivion. For, as Dr. Eugene Carson Blake has emphasized: "A government with mounting
tax problems cannot be expected to keep its hands off the
wealth of a rich church forever. The economic power that
will increasingly be wielded by ever richer churches threatens
to produce not only envy, hatred, or resentment of nonmem-
bers, but also to distract the purposes of the church members
and leaders themselves."

APPENDIX

Some representative policy statements
on churches and taxes.
(Excerpts)

I. Statements of Protestant Groups

1. National Council of Churches' Study Conference Report (1964)

2. Methodist Church Study Commission Report (1968)

3. United Presbyterian Church in the U.S.A. Special Committee Report (1963)

4. American Lutheran Church Policy Statement (1966)

5. Guild of St. Ives Report (1967)

6. Baptist Joint Committee Conference Report (1960)

II. Statements of the Catholic Press

1. "Taxing the Churches," *America* (1967)

2. "Churches and Taxes," *Ave Maria* (1964)

3. "Churches and Public Financial Reports," *America* (1967)

4. "Religious Tax Exemptions and the First Amendment," *The Catholic World* (1965)

Report of the National Study Conference on Church and State

(Conducted under authorization of the General Board of the National Council of Churches of Christ in the U.S.A.)
(1964)

SECTION SIX

Taxation, Exemption, and Deduction in Relation to Churches:

The diversity of forms of taxation make difficult any generalizations concerning sound policies for tax exemption for religious institutions. However, we believe that certain forms of tax exemption for such institutions may be supported on two grounds:

1) Religious institutions perform useful functions in society which are properly recognized by the state, and the state should not place the existence of such institutions in jeopardy through taxation. On the one level, such institutions are usually charitable in a sense broader than their religious definitions. On another level, they perform the critically important task of cultivating and transmitting ideas and values. Without such institutions performing these functions, any society, particularly one with democratic objectives, might be seriously crippled.

2) In some instances tax exemption for religious and other nonprofit institutions minimizes double taxation.*

---

* Thirty-one delegates wished to register dissent to what they felt was the ambiguous use of the term "double taxation" and were permitted to do so by majority vote.

These theoretical premises of tax exemption do not justify either of the following:

1) the exemption from taxation of religious institutions to the extent of their cost to the government;

2) the preferential treatment of any or all religious institutions over other institutions which primarily function charitably or in the cultivation and transmission of ideas and values.

Since tax exemptions such as these lack theoretical justification government has no duty to provide them.

These observations are offered as a contribution to public discussion of these issues. In offering them, no special privileges are claimed on the basis of religious beliefs. We also offer a special word of caution to ourselves and others within the churches: We are especially impressed by the need for churches to guard their freedom and the integrity of their witness by not being beholden for their support to persons and agencies not committed to the Gospel. Government agencies are not and should not be so committed. Our churches must look for their support to the dedicated and disciplined stewardship of their members.

The following specific recommendations are offered as illustrative applications of these principles:

A) We recommend that employment tax laws, federal and state, be made fully applicable to churches.

B) We favor income tax deductions for contributions for eleemosynary purposes, including religious purposes.

C) We approve exemption from gift taxes and death and succession taxes of contributions for eleemosynary purposes, including religious purposes.

D) We recommend that exemptions for churches from excise taxes be eliminated.

E) We express disapproval of the practice of exempting the unrelated taxable business income of church bodies as that term is used in federal income tax laws.

F) We express disapproval of granting an exemption from taxation of allowances to ministers of the gospel by way of housing or substitutes therefor, as provided currently in Section 107 of the Internal Revenue Code.

We further recommend that this study conference call on the churches to examine their practice in respect to tax exempt status of properties they own in order to move toward taking a proper share of tax liabilities on such properties, and that the National Council of Churches call upon its member communions to implement this study.

[AUTHOR'S NOTE: The conference report notes: "The conference speaks for itself and not for the Council·nor the appointing bodies. It neither commits nor represents the Council or these bodies. . . . The composition of the conference was as follows: 245 delegates designated by member communions of the National Council of Churches; 36 delegates designated by nonmember communions, including the American Lutheran Church, the Lutheran Church—Missouri Synod, and the Southern Baptist Convention; 22 delegates designated by Councils of Churches; 14 observers designated by the National Catholic Welfare Conference; nine observers designated by the Synagogue Council of America, the National Association of Evangelicals, and the Church of Christ, Scientist; 17 consultants invited by the Department of Religious Liberty; and 21 staff advisers designated by units of the National Council of Churches. The total number of delegates was thus 303, plus 61 nonvoting participants." A subsequent report (1967) by an NCC Ad Hoc Study Committee on Tax Exemption of Churches had neither been acted upon nor released for publication by the governmental relations unit of the NCC at this writing.]

Report of a Study Commission on the Methodist Church and Church-Government Relations

(Presented to the General Conference of the United Methodist Church, 1968)

In examining the factors that influence relations between churches and governments, the context of present conditions and recent developments among the churches must be considered. One development is the far-reaching transformation which has occurred in the organizational aspects of churches. . . . The once relatively simple forms of association for the promotion of religious interests have evolved into exceedingly complex organizations. . . .

Churches have acquired a large amount of economic and social power. They employ labor, provide social services, and operate educational institutions; they sponsor recreation, entertainment, and cultural enterprises; they are landlords as well as tenants; and they collect, expend, and invest money, as well as administer retirement and pension systems. Clearly churches now have the power to make economic and social decisions that vitally affect the lives and welfare of millions of people. No government can completely ignore the manner in which this economic and social power is exercised by church officials. . . .

One context in which issues regarding the proper relationship between churches and governments have arisen during the past decade is the exemption of religious groups

from various types of tax liability. Such issues have arisen in
part because of a lack of a generally accepted rationale for
government tax exemption policies and practices.

Throughout the course of American history, federal,
state, and local tax laws and policies have extended to religious societies the valuable privilege of exemption from tax
liabilities. Such exemptions are found in statutes and ordi-
nances relating to taxes on property, income, inheritances, estates, gifts, sales, admissions, and the like. . . . Anson Phelps
Stokes was probably correct when he observed, in *Church
and State in the United States,* that the "greatest single help
given by the State to the Church in this country" is the tax
exemption. . . .

Many nonprofit charitable organizations other than
churches and their affiliated agencies are granted the privilege
of exemption from certain kinds of tax liability. If a general
rationale is formulated to justify the tax exemption policies
of federal, state, and local governments, that rationale will
have implications for churches and their affiliated institutions.

Undoubtedly the privilege of being exempt from tax
liability is an aid to churches. Whether this aid is direct or
indirect does not appear to have any great economic significance insofar as churches are concerned. It remains yet to be
determined that the particular public policy grounds upon
which American courts have sustained such tax exemption
can or will have a significant effect on the mission of
churches in contemporary American society. Therefore, the
issue of proper relations between churches and governments,
in the context of tax exemption, is actually a matter of the
particular kind and degree of tax exemption. The crucial
question is "What form and degree of exemption of churches
from tax liability constitute an impermissible relationship between religious societies and governments?"

A Statement Concerning
Church-Government Relations
and Tax Exemption

I

We believe that where governments, for any reason of public policy, create or recognize a general category of non-profit charitable organizations for purposes of tax exemption, churches ought to be included in such general category. If it is the policy of governments to help nonprofit charitable organizations through the granting of immunities from tax liabilities, to omit churches from the application of that policy would be an unwarranted discrimination against religious interests and, conceivably, might amount to a restraint on free exercise of religion. The wisdom or lack of wisdom of such a government policy, however, ought to be determined on grounds more inclusive than its effects on religious interests.

II

We do not perceive any justification for government policies and practices which accord special privileges to or provide differential treatment of churches in the matter of exemption from tax liability. It is our conviction that the special treatment accorded to "churches and conventions or associations of churches" with respect to exclusion of their unrelated business income from federal income taxation ought to be discontinued. Nor do we believe there is any justification for relieving churches of the obligation of reporting their earnings in the same manner that is required of other charitable organizations. We are persuaded that discrimination in *favor* of churches in governmental taxation is just as pernicious as discrimination *against* religious groups.

It is incumbent upon churches to consider at least the following factors in determining their response to the granting of immunity from property taxes:

1) Responsibility to make appropriate contribution, in lieu of taxes, for essential services provided by government.
2) The danger that churches become so dependent upon government that they compromise their integrity or fail to exert their critical influence upon public policy.

III

We support the abolition of all special privileges accorded to members of the clergy in American tax laws and regulations, and call upon the churches to deal with the consequent financial implications for their ministers. Conversely, we believe that all forms of discrimination against members of the clergy in American tax legislation and administrative regulations should be discontinued. We do not believe that the status of an individual under ecclesiastical law or practice ought to be made the basis of governmental action either granting or withholding a tax benefit.

Report of the Special Committee on Relations Between Church and State in the U.S.A.

United Presbyterian Church in the U.S.A.
(Adopted by the 175th General Assembly, May 1963)

Tax exemptions for religious agencies:

The church has no theological ground for laying any claim upon the state for special favors. The church must regard special status or favored position as a hindrance to the fulfilling of its mission. As a matter of contemporary fact, various levels of government give the church and many of its agencies a wide variety of tax exemptions. The church would find it difficult to obtain the abrogation of these laws and administrative practices. In the face of this situation, two points need to be made abundantly clear by the church, the first directed to itself and its membership and the second to the state and its representatives.

First, to itself as the agent of the ministry of Jesus Christ to the world, the church should know that it renders its witness ambiguous by its continued acceptance of special privileges from the state in the form of tax exemptions. Second, the state should know that it may not expect from the church in return for favors extended of its own free will, any *quid pro quo* in the form of a muting of the church's prophetic voice, nor should the state expect the church to accept the role of an uncritical instrument of support for the state's programs, or of any other conscious dilution of its supreme loyalty to Jesus Christ.

In view of these considerations, the Special Committee on Church and State *recommends* that:

a) United Presbyterians study the nature of our Church's involvement in economic activity and seek ways by which it can begin the process of extricating itself from the position of being obligated, or seeming to be obligated, to the state by virtue of special tax privileges extended to it.

b) The United Presbyterian Church carefully examine its national and local related business enterprises to assure itself that under present tax laws these enterprises are not unfairly competitive with secular businesses operating in the same fields. To this end the Committee suggests that the General Assembly direct the Stated Clerk to canvass the boards, agencies, institutions, and judicatories to determine the extent of their economic involvement subject to tax exemption and to report to the General Council of the United Presbyterian Church, which is to report to a future General Assembly.

c) The United Presbyterian Church continue efforts to obtain repeal of the section of the Internal Revenue Code that allows "churches and church organizations" exemption from the corporate income tax on profits of businesses unrelated to the purpose or activity of the church or church organization.

d) Congregations be encouraged to take the initiative in making contributions to local communities, in lieu of taxes, in recognition of police, fire, and other services provided by local government. This consideration commends itself especially to well established and financially stable churches and particularly to those in communities where tax problems are developing due, in part, to the increase in exempted properties for all purposes—educational, governmental, charitable, and religious. Those congregations which thus make voluntary contributions in lieu of taxes should not expect consideration or special favor in return. . . .

Church-State Relations in the U.S.A.

(Accepted by the General Convention
of the American Lutheran Church
as a statement of policy and conviction,
October 1966.)

Numerous issues affecting church-state relations, the place of religion in public life, and the recognition of deity by government, have entered the arena of public debate. The issues have arisen in large part because of the increased heterogeneity of the American population, the acceptance of religious pluralism, the extension of governmental influence into nearly every phase of life, the need for additional tax revenues, and the difficulties for the churches in meeting the growing demands and complexities of their programs of health, education, and welfare.

We recognize that Scripture gives only guidelines, not blueprints, for determining church-state relations. The charge given the church to make disciples of all men (Matt. 28: 16-20), the power given government to support good and to curb evil (Rom. 13:1-7), the separation between that which is owed to God and to government (Matt. 22:15-22), and the direction of the Christian's influence in society (Mark 12:28-34) remain basic for all generations. The specific ways of fostering and protecting these essentials, however, may and do differ from age to age and from nation to nation. . . .

In its practical operation the American heritage generally has embodied a flexible pattern of cooperation between church and state in providing for persons such services as are deemed to be in the public interest and for the good of the community. Neither indifference, nor hostility, nor a wall of separation but a flexible friendly cooperation to achieve what is agreed as being for the common good has marked church-state relationships in America. This has been especially true in the areas of education, welfare services, and ministries to persons in institutions and the armed forces.

Danger exists for both church and state in too-close an identification with the programs of each. Governmental grants, loans, and other forms of assistance to religious institutions indeed may enable the churches the more effectively to serve the needs of an expanding society. Such governmental assistance may also, on the other side, compromise the religious character of the institution and jeopardize its essential integrity. What may be good for government may be harmful to the church, or vice versa. One or a few religious groups may be strengthened to the disadvantage of others. Governmental policies may be determined by one or another strong religious group to its own temporal advantage. . . .

Policies Respecting Taxation:

Tax policies should encourage personal contributions to voluntary, not-for-profit, organizations of a charitable, health, educational, or religious character. The community needs strong organizations of this type, alike for their positive values, to avoid total reliance upon governmental agencies, and for the mutually healthy and corrective influence between governmental and voluntary agencies. The freedom of the individual citizen to exercise his personal philanthropy and generously to support constructive voluntary enterprises of his own choice ought to be protected in the public interest.

Tax exemption of church buildings owned and used directly and solely for worship, educational, and eleemosynary purposes is a sound exercise of public policy. It recognizes the contributions the church and its institutions make to community life. To levy upon churches nondiscriminatory charges for municipal services such as water, sewage, police, and fire protection we believe is an action consistent with sound public policy. We believe that the churches should be willing to accept equitable taxation of parsonages and other dwellings owned by churches, associations of churches, or religious orders in which their staff members reside.

Churches owning properties and conducting business not exclusively and solely essential to their religious, charitable, or educational ministry ought to be subject to tax laws and policies equally applicable to those governing profit-seeking individuals, partnerships, and corporations.

A Report on Churches and Taxation

The Guild of St. Ives
(Organization of Episcopal lawyers and clerics, New York)
(1967)

. . . The total wealth of organized religion and of other tax-exempt institutions is growing while the needs of government, particularly at the local level, are increasing. Tax burdens are also increasing, and would probably be increasing faster except for the vague limits of political expediency. With growing tax burdens producing increasing discomfort and discontent, it is not surprising that the tax shelters accorded organized religion (among others) by existing tax laws have already come under criticism. This criticism seems bound to increase, since none of the above trends appears to be reversible in the immediate future.

As a practical matter, then, the question of taxation and religion should be reexamined. Even if political pressure to end present tax exemptions were not increasing, religious organizations themselves have a moral obligation to reexamine the question under current conditions. . . .

The majority recognize that there is a minority of one who does not concur with the majority insofar as the majority favor any preferential treatment for any religious institution. This minority also questions the wisdom of many of the charitable and educational exemptions which are outside the scope of this report.

Property taxes:

The undersigned believe that real and personal property

owned by religious institutions should be subject to taxation
to the extent that it is used for business purposes in either
actual or potential competition with secular persons, or if it
is unused and not definitely committed in the immediate
future to some exempt use. Such property appears to constitute a significant portion of the "wealth" of organized religion which is currently subject to criticism. Such tax treatment is believed to accord, at least generally, with existing
practice.

The majority believe that real and personal property
owned by religious institutions which is used for educational,
charitable, and other social purposes should not be taxed any
more or less than such property would be taxed if owned by
secular organizations. In short, there is no reason to deny
church schools, hospitals, and other charities the same tax
treatment they would receive if they were owned and operated the same way by someone else.

The majority believe that property owned by religious
organizations which is used for religious purposes should remain exempt from taxation. This category primarily encom-
passes churches, chapels, parish houses, and synagogues. They
are believed to constitute the greatest part of the "wealth" of
most religious congregations in this country, a significant
number of which are only marginal operations in an economic sense. The repeal of this exemption, resulting in repeated annual assessments which would bear no necessary
relationship to current cash flow, would constitute a major
hardship to organized religion as we know it today in its
broadest and most basic sense. We believe that legislators
should continue this exemption to religious institutions in
recognition of their overall beneficial role in our society.
These tax exemptions have, historically, been accorded to
organized religion (as well as education and charity) as a
public recognition of public services rendered. We are all in
agreement that this exemption should not extend to taxes,

charges, or assessments which are rationally measured by benefits demonstrably conferred upon the property—paving assessments, utility charges, etc.

Income taxes:

Present effective corporate tax rates (most religious organizations are corporations) are roughly 48 per cent on interest and other income, 7.2 per cent on dividend income, and 25 per cent (maximum) on profits from the sale of business assets, property, or securities held for more than six months. Expenses reasonably incurred to produce such income are normally deducted before the taxes are applied. The undersigned are fully aware that such taxation of such income of religious organizations will have a serious financial effect on the economy of organized religion. For this reason, we suggest that any new taxation of income of religious organizations be phased in progressively over a five- to ten-year period. Such a time of transition should give religious organizations a better opportunity to adjust to their changed circumstances.

Income from unrelated businesses owned by religious organizations is not now taxed (except to the extent such businesses are operated as independent, taxable corporations). In this respect, religious organizations are favored over even educational and charitable ones. The undersigned disagree with such treatment in principle. Such unrelated businesses are operated in actual or potential competition with secular businesses and should, we feel, be accorded similar tax treatment.

The majority also believe that religious organizations should recognize the unfairness of their competitive business advantage. To reduce this advantage, religious organizations should operate their businesses in the corporate form, thereby subjecting those businesses to the same income taxes as their competitors.

The undersigned are of more than one mind on the subject of what is sometimes called "passive" investment income. About half would exempt such income (as is presently done) on the grounds 1) that such income is normally spent for religious and charitable purposes, and 2) that the tax exemption has no adverse competitive effect on others. About half of the undersigned believe that such "passive" investment income should be taxed. While some who favor such taxation believe it should be at ordinary corporate rates, a number believe that such a tax 1) should, perhaps, be at lower than generally applied rates in recognition of the religious, educational, and charitable uses to which such income is put, or 2) should, perhaps, be applied only to income in excess of a certain specified amount so as not to penalize religious organizations with relatively modest investment incomes, or 3) should, perhaps, in some other way be tailored to prevent the future accumulation of investments as a result of tax-free income, yet permit present uses of such income from current investments on a tax-free basis. Those who accept the principle of taxation of investment income do so because they recognize that this is the area in which the "wealth" of organized religion is growing fastest, and which is subject to the most pervasive and persuasive criticism.

Whatever wealth organized religion may possess, of course, is mainly attributable to contributions which would be tax deductible (and tax exempt to the recipient) under today's tax laws. Viewing the question of income taxation from this starting point may be helpful in understanding the views of those who would tax "passive" investment income.

The original contribution, though tax exempt, does not in and of itself permanently remove any funds from what might be called the taxable wealth of the nation. To the extent the contribution is utilized to meet operating expenses of the religious organization (salaries, maintenance, etc.) it is quickly returned to the taxable wealth. To the extent it is used to build churches and other exempt structures, its amount, for what we believe are good reasons, is removed from the taxable wealth of the nation. To the extent such a contribution is turned into an investment and/or business operation, it is probably returned to the taxable wealth of the nation, but only in exchange for other property which is simultaneously removed from that taxable wealth. Those of us who would tax investment income believe that any increased value of such investment or business operation upon sale, and the income derived therefrom, should remain part of the taxable wealth for two reasons. *First,* such investments and businesses are uses to which contributions are frequently put only in the absence of more pressing and immediate religious needs. *Second,* it is here that pyramiding of such investments poses the most serious threat of erosion of the national tax base.

One exception should be made to the above. To the extent such business income or investments are realized or owned by educational or charitable organizations and would not be taxed if owned or operated by secular educational or charitable institutions, there should be a tax exemption. Again, we can see no reason why the tax treatment of church and secular-owned educational and religious institutions should not be the same, though we have obviously touched upon an even broader question of tax policy here.

Sales, Franchise, License, Excise, and Other Similar Taxes:

Miscellaneous taxes, such as sales, license, and excise taxes, are normally imposed in relatively nominal amounts, and frequently are imposed to regulate, supervise, or facilitate the commercial activity with respect to which they are imposed. Subject to the above-stated caveat that church-sponsored educational and charitable activities should be treated the same as any other such activities, we see no pressing reason why any exemptions should be granted in this area.

Salaries Paid by Religious Institutions:

These are generally taxed the same as any other salaries earned in our society, and we see no reason for change.

Deductions for Gifts to Religious Institutions and Organizations:

Within limits, these gifts are generally deductible just as are contributions to educational and charitable institutions. Since we believe that the social value of organized religion to our society is at least comparable to that of educational institutions and of charitable organizations, and that it is appropriate to encourage such contributions, we propose no change in this regard.

One Final Recommendation:

Present tax laws, particularly real property tax laws, may limit exemptions in various ways—e.g., to the extent of actual religious use of the property in question. It has come to our attention that certain religious institutions, like many businesses, take a somewhat relaxed view of such limitations. Specifically, they tend to be lax in reporting changed uses of property which would remove their exemptions, and wait for the taxing authorities to catch up to the change. It is respectfully submitted that the morals of the marketplace are not appropriate to organized religion, that the public which has given organized religion its favored tax status has a right to expect better, and that organized religion should in all good conscience offer it better. It is therefore recommended that the various financial officers of the religious establishment voluntarily undertake a program of periodic self-policing of all claimed tax exemptions, and that they be directed by higher ecclesiastical authorities to do so.

Conference Report

Baptist Joint Committee on Public Affairs
(September, 1960)

The fourth annual Religious Liberty Conference, sponsored by the Baptist Joint Committee on Public Affairs, met in Washington, D.C., September 6-9 at the Calvary Baptist Church. Eighty-five Baptist leaders from four national fellowships composed the membership of the conference. Among them were executive secretaries, editors, pastors, administrators, lawyers, and Baptist agency representatives. The four Baptist bodies represented were the American Baptist Convention, the Southern Baptist Convention, Baptist General Conference, and North American Baptist General Conference. . . .

Church Property:

Conference opinion: Although the New Testament does not offer any specific precedent for tax exemption of church property as here defined, the majority feels that no conflict with New Testament principles is involved in the concept of tax exemption.

It is the consensus that the present practice of allowing churches tax exemption on their real property is not affecting adversely their freedom to enjoy and propagate the gospel. However, there is deep concern about the future as churches increase in wealth and property, which from history raises the question of the development of such attitudes as anticlericalism.

Inasmuch as religious freedom requires that no favoritism be shown by the Government to any religious group it is essential that we maintain vigilance to see that legislative action always embodies the principle of equitable application of the tax exemption.

Minority opinion: There was a strong minority opinion that any form of tax exemption for churches injures the future of the freedom of the churches. . . .

Conference opinion: Tax exemption does impose passive religious participation, but not in the same way as if tax money were being used directly to support religious institutions.

It was suggested that studies might be made to determine the costs of various municipal services furnished the churches, to provide the basis for possible payment by churches for such services. . . .

Conference opinion: The test of whether any type of church property should be exempted from local real estate tax should be the manner in which it is used. Property which is not used for the stated religious purposes of the church, and which is in competition with the business establishments of the community might properly be taxed, even though the income from such activities is devoted wholly to the work of the church.

It was the consensus of the group that parsonages should be taxed. In some cases where they are largely used for church activities justification for exemption might be found.

Denominational offices should be exempt inasmuch as they are a valid extension of the work of the local church.

No agreement was reached in the matter of taxes on publishing firms. The majority seemed to feel they should be afforded tax exemption except as their operations involve them in competition with commercial enterprises.

It was felt that parking lots should be exempted unless they are used for the production of income.

Income-producing real estate should be taxed. . . .

Church Businesses:

Question: Is your group averse to the current "unrelated business income" privilege for churches?

Conference opinion: Yes, because federal income tax exemption tends to 1) encourage promotion of or participation in secular business to the detriment of the principal mission of the church; 2) to encourage morally unjustifiable arrangements with businessmen or companies to reduce their income taxes; 3) discourage financial support of church activities by voluntary contributions of all members.

Question: Do your arguments and evaluations apply also to "related business income" such as the *profits* from book or literature business?

Conference opinion: No, because subjection of church-related business to the burden of federal income tax 1) would tend to reduce the productiveness of business of the type which actively promotes the spread of the gospel; 2) would tend to curtail an important phase of the church mission; 3) cannot be justified by the argument that church-related business should be on the same tax basis as other business because such church-related business is not competitive with secular business. . . .

Conference opinion: By unrelated business income we mean earnings from businesses which have no direct connection with the religious purposes of the church regardless of how that income is used. To determine whether income (not gifts) is church-related for the purpose of exemption from the payment of income tax the sources of the income should be examined.

The basic criterion should be the source from which the income is derived rather than the use to which it is put. All income from religious activities or from the sale or lease of articles of religious character such as religious literature, pictures, music, motion pictures, and all income received by one religious organization from another religious organization should be exempt from income taxation.

It is our judgment that our Baptist insights point to the principle that income earned by securities owned by a religious organization or agency would not be exempt from taxation. We recognize that the implications of this principle are not fully clear at this time, and we believe that the continued study and application of this concept should receive the early and careful attention of the responsible organizations of our several Baptist bodies.

Minority opinion: We suggest that consideration also be given to the tax rate which should be applicable to income of the character that is to be taxable. Churches are incorporated to hold title to property for nonprofit purposes. Business firms are incorporated for a different purpose, to make a profit. As a result tax rates are different. . . .

Conference opinion: We favor using our influence to bring about a revision of the Internal Revenue Code to remove the special preferred position of churches and place them on a par with other nonprofit benevolent institutions and agencies. . . .

Conference opinion: We suggest that the Baptist Joint Committee on Public Affairs seek to call the attention of our cooperating Baptist bodies to the problems in this area and the many apparent abuses of the principle of separation of church and state as it relates to tax responsibility. Also, we suggest that it seek to foster constructive approaches to the solution of these problems.

One table questioned the preferential tax treatment for individuals on the ground of their religious occupation: We advocate such changes in the income tax laws as will abolish the preferential treatment which ministers, nuns, priests, rabbis, and certain other professional religious leaders have in relation to other citizens. . . .

Church Stewardship:

Question: Do we have anything to fear from the present provisions for "deduction" of church contributions when filing income tax returns?

Conference opinion: It is our conviction that we do not need to fear from such provisions for deduction. It is our strong feeling that the Government is not concerned with the motivation or quality of the individual's stewardship. The Church of Christ has the responsibility of trying to develop this quality of an individual's stewardship. But we do deplore the tendency in some quarters to use the deduction idea in order to collect funds for church purposes. We believe that this is a part of the secularization process going on in America today.

It is further reported that we fear the temptation of misrepresentation of charitable giving as a result of our present deduction provisions.

Minority opinion: Fear was further expressed by some that the present policy of tax deductions materially affects our position on separation, as it evidences the creeping subsidization of churches and church organizations by government.

Question: Do we have anything to fear from the repeal of "deductions" or from their extension as a benefit to education?

Conference opinion: We are not concerned or "afraid" of the results that would follow should the deductions for churches be repealed. If this is the right thing to do, then the Lord will provide for our churches. Such a repeal of deductions would probably affect our education institutions most adversely. To be sure, a jolt would be felt in our churches. But it would be the Government's decision to repeal the deduction for churches—not ours.

We have no fear of such repeal for we believe that, in the long pull following such repeal, there would be temporary difficulties as people made their adjustments to a new approach in the support of their institutions. In the long run the adjustment would be made, we believe. . . .

Conference opinion: It is our conclusion that the church personnel, in regard to a position of privilege in tax-related problems, should stand before the government as any other citizen. . . .

Minority opinion: There was a minority report to the effect that some provision should be made for exemptions that we now have under the law to avoid paying sales taxes for articles purchased for church use.

We hold certain privilege tax exemptions, provided by law to religious organizations, are simply a recognition of the inherent value of religion to the state, and are right.

The amount and kind should have constant study and control. Additional privileges should not be sought.

Baptists should oppose special provision for churches and church personnel in items like excise taxes, legally established rates for travel, water, power, etc. This differs from deduction on personal income tax in that it involves an organizational or corporate relationship rather than an individual one. Hence the tension toward the ideal of separation of church and state should be tighter. The argument that the power to tax is the power to destroy does not hold here because of the variable factor in these taxes being attached to services rendered or materials purchased. It seems unlikely that such taxes could ever be damaging to a church's existence or autonomy. . . .

Taxing the Churches:
The Law and the Facts*

The factual and legal sloppiness that has characterized current discussions over taxing the churches makes it necessary to recall certain truths about American law. For example, it is fatuous for anyone to assert that churches do not have to pay real estate taxes on the property they own. They do—unless they also use the property, exclusively or almost so, for religious purposes. That may be so, it will be argued, but churches do not have to pay the federal income tax on rents they receive from property they own but lease for commercial or other nonreligious purposes.

The argument neglects to mention that, on this point, Harvard, Yale, and the Ford Foundation are in exactly the same position as the churches. Exemption of rental income is part of the general tax advantage shared by all exempt organizations. People who would take this advantage away from the churches ought to explain why they would keep it for other organizations.

The same is to be said of the proposal to tax the investment income of the churches. There might be some merit in the idea, but why concentrate on the churches? The investment income of all exempt organizations is free from taxation. If we need the money badly enough to tax St. Patrick's Cathedral, Riverside Church, and Temple Emmanu-El, we

* Reprinted with permission from *America* (June 3, 1967), The National Catholic Weekly Review, 106 W. 56th Street, New York, N.Y. 10019, ©1967 America Press, Inc.

certainly need the money badly enough to tax labor unions, pension funds, and the opulent family foundations.

The one area in which the churches have an advantage over some—but not all—exempt organizations lies in the operation of unrelated businesses. On the face of it, no exempt organization should be allowed to operate an unrelated business tax-free. Unless Congress can come up with a satisfactory reason for maintaining this peculiar exemption, the exemption ought to be phased out of our law.

Much more could be said about the realities and complexities of tax exemptions in general and of the tax status of churches in particular. Rather than get lost in technicalities, however, it will be well to turn attention to two fundamental financial questions. How much money would be realized if the income tax exemption of churches were abolished? How much money would be realized if the real estate tax exemption of churches were abolished?

Nobody knows for certain, but it is a pretty good guess that not a single penny would be realized from the abolition of the income tax exemption and that comparatively little would be realized from the abolition of the real estate exemption.

For an organization to have to pay an income tax, it must have, not an income, but a taxable income in excess of the statutory exclusions and deductions. It seems likely that the greatest part of the annual income of the churches is derived from current free-will offerings. These would be excludable from taxable income of the churches because they are gifts. From their sources of income which would be classified as taxable, churches would be entitled to deduct their ordinary and necessary expenses. In view of many Supreme Court decisions in the area of Church and State, the Internal Revenue Service would have to allow churches the greatest latitude in determining what their ordinary and necessary religious expenses would be. It is wholly to be expected that every church would use up its taxable income in such expenses, with the result that churches would not have to pay any income tax at all.

So far as real estate taxation is concerned, most church property is entitled to exemption on a double ground, both as devoted to a religious undertaking and as devoted to a school, hospital, orphanage, or some other charitable enterprise. It is only the houses of worship that would be substantially affected by imposition of the real estate tax. How should such property be assessed? Not on the basis of the value of neighboring commercial or industrial property, because church property cannot be used for such purposes. In all fairness, a separate basis of assessment would have to be found, one related to the economic value of the religious use of land. Since, despite the jokes, religion really isn't a profit-making affair, a fair assessment of property devoted to houses of worship probably would produce comparatively little in the way of real estate taxes.

Ultimately, the most important question is not how much money the churches have, but what they are doing with it. Part of the reason that religious organizations are given exemptions from the tax laws is that they are believed to be performing a public service. If the churches wish to keep that belief alive, they would do well to foster it not only by performing their good works in the light of day, but also by making regular, professional, and informative financial reports.

Churches and Taxes*

When Congress finally gets around to serious delibera-
tion on the tax cut, we are likely to hear some blistering
speeches on the number of dollars eluding the government
bite through the operation of tax-exempt foundations. (It
was recently reported that the assets of these foundations last
year added up to $14.5 billion.)

We shall also hear some criticism—much more cautious
criticism, to be sure—about the tax dollars getting away from
the government through businesses owned by religious
groups. (A few months ago the *Wall Street Journal* carried a
something-ought-to-be-done report on these operations. It
listed church-owned holdings as diverse as hotels, super-
markets and the mortgage on Billy Sol Estes' home.)

If there should exist a Congressional district with a pre-
dominantly atheistic population, its Congressman might
launch a crusade against all tax exemptions for religious organizations. But it's not likely that a majority of this Congress will push for wholesale revisions which would seriously
disrupt the operations of all organized religious groups.

However, a few points should be made.

First, administrators of church property should begin to
concern themselves about those holdings which are clearly
tax dodges. If a business is not related to the spiritual, charitable purposes of the church; if the tax exemption amounts
to an unfair competitive business advantage; if the "donation" to the church isn't really a *donation* at all, but only a
way in which the donor can preserve or improve his own

* Reprinted with permission from *Ave Maria* (January 18, 1964), ©1964
by Ave Maria Press, Congregation of the Holy Cross, Notre Dame, Indiana.

financial situation—if these conditions are present, then the ecclesiastical administrators should be concerned about scandal and about responsibility to the nation.

Second, it should be remembered by Congressional speechmakers and by others that most of the churches, in their administration of these funds, are simply serving as agents for a very widespread membership. The taxpayers of the nation are basically the same people who are contributing to the charitable and devotional works of the church. Restrictions that place harsh financial burdens on the churches are likely to curtail social services (which will fall to the responsibility of government), or they will place additional expenses on the church members. And these are the people who were supposed to benefit from tax reductions.

Finally, we accept the fact that huge networks of church-sponsored institutions resting on the shaky financial structure of tax loopholes is a situation far from desirable.

We would recommend the initiation of informal discussions between Church spokesmen and government officials to begin a gradual solution of a situation which could grow into a serious problem for all the churches.

Churches and Public Financial Reports*

With the end of the fiscal year at hand, countless organizations are preparing financial reports. Catholic institutions are no exception. Not all of them, of course, operate on a July-June fiscal year; but every institution, religious or secular, has to take periodic stock of its finances if it is to survive. What differentiates Catholic financial reports from their secular counterparts is that most of the Catholic reports are carefully hidden from the public.

The secular world of business, it is true, has its own jealously guarded financial secrets. Law and custom, however, have long since compelled businesses to make basic disclosures to the public. The balance sheet and income-expense statement are standard features of American commercial life. Each year the major American corporations spend a small fortune designing, printing and distributing their annual reports.

Much less lavish, but still most carefully done, are the annual reports of such nonprofit giants as the Ford Foundation. If anyone wants to know what the Ford Foundation says it is worth and what it did with its money last year, the answers are not hard to find. Similar financial reports are issued by many of the major nonprofit, nonreligious institutions in the United States. Public accountability is accepted by these institutions as a simple corollary of the dedication of their funds to public use.

With religious organizations, however, financial secrecy

* Reprinted with permission from *America* (July 1, 1967), The National Catholic Weekly Review, 106 W. 56th Street, New York, N.Y. 10019, ©1967 America Press, Inc.

remains the rule. Many Protestant organizations and some Catholic and Jewish organizations issue financial reports; but not enough follow this practice to provide a sound basis for estimating the assets and liabilities, costs and income, of organized religion in America. And it must be confessed that, of the three major religious groups in the United States, the Catholics seem the most secretive.

In part, this secrecy is a hangover from the days when, theoretically at least, the clergy were the ruling body and the laity the submissive sheep. The People of God were fed, but not informed. In part, however, the nonpublication of religious data was also the result of the legal exemption of religious organizations from reporting requirements. This exemption was one facet of Church-State separation: as far as possible, the government kept out of the financial affairs of the churches.

Today, however, there are serious reasons for breaking the habit of secrecy. Church funds, after all, are trust funds— not just a trust for the Church itself conceived as an organization, but a trust for the People of God and for all men. One of the most fundamental rights of a beneficiary is the right to an accounting. Without that, the beneficiary is at the mercy of the trustee. And the institutional Church's mercy is not always gentle, much less efficient.

Undoubtedly, there are some special problems to be solved in the composition of annual financial reports for churches. The problems, however, are no more difficult than those confronting American business in its efforts to make itself financially comprehensible. It takes a certain amount of skill to understand the annual report of a major corporation like General Motors. It will also take skill, as well as curiosity, to learn anything from the annual financial report of the Catholic Church in the United States.

Financial reports to the clergy, laity and public would

be an important symbol of the trusteeship of religious congregations and of the hierarchy. Such trusteeship needs to be emphasized today, when murmurs about Church wealth increase daily. It is time to make clear what the Church is doing with what it has.

Religious Tax Exemptions
and the First Amendment*

"Why should I pay more taxes, while moral and ethical leaders, as they call themselves, get off tax-free?" Thus did Mrs. Madalyn Murray, a professed atheist, summarize the issue as she brought suit in Maryland to challenge the tax exemption of religious institutions. Mrs. Murray is well-known as the victorious plaintiff in the recent Supreme Court decision banning the recitation of the Lord's Prayer and the reading of the Bible as a religious exercise in the public schools.

The problem of the religious tax exemption is of more than passing interest. With increasing pressure to provide more services for their citizens, most state and local governments are re-examining their tax structure and searching about for new ways of raising public revenue. At the same time, the sensitivity of segments of the American people to involvements of religion in public life has led to an evaluation of traditional practices and policies favoring religion in the light of recent Supreme Court interpretations of the establishment clause of the First Amendment. . . .

The observations in this article will be confined primarily to exemptions from taxes on real property, although many of the conclusions will apply equally to other forms of tax exemption. The emphasis will be placed chiefly on the constitutional issues involved in tax exemptions rather than on public policy arguments. . . .

* John J. Regan, C.M., dean of the Colleges of Liberal Arts and Sciences, St. John's University, in *The Catholic World* (May 1965). © 1965 by *The Catholic World*, Glen Rock, N.J. 07452. Abridged and reprinted with permission.

94 THE RELIGION BUSINESS

The Supreme Court has not ruled on the issue whether such exemptions constitute a violation of the establishment clause. The Court had the opportunity to do so in 1956 and again in 1962 in appeals taken from the decisions of the California and Rhode Island Supreme Courts, but it dismissed these appeals on the ground that they did not raise substantial federal questions. It is arguable that such dismissals meant that these exemptions raised no real issue with respect to the First Amendment, but it would be hazardous to say that these dismissals give a definitive answer to the problem. . . .

The case against the religious tax exemption rests on a rigid interpretation of the "no-aid" principle set forth by Justice Black in *Everson*. . . . Taken literally, this principle means that the federal government and the states must not permit any form of financial support for religious activities, even on a nonsectarian basis. The fact that such aid is part of a general program of governmental support extended indiscriminately to activities with secular purposes is irrelevant; aid must be denied to the religious portion of such activities. Thus it would make no difference that the exemption for churches is part of the over-all exemption for property of all nonprofit organizations serving charitable purposes. . . .

As cogent as . . . arguments against the exemptions may appear, supporters of the exemptions find them out of step with the latest trends in Supreme Court interpretations of the religion clauses. The arguments are also relatively unsophisticated in their treatment of so delicate an area as the First Amendment. . . .

The principle of "religious neutrality" as the working norm in government-religion relations provides justification for most, if not all, of the religious tax exemptions now permitted. . . . The question thus is: Do tax exemptions for religious institutions have a secular, legislative purpose and is their effect primarily secular in nature? To answer this question a distinction must be drawn between the various types of activity engaged in by churches and religious institutions. Such activity is frequently concerned with education, hospitals, and charitable work for various underprivileged groups in society. Not only secular private agencies but government itself is also concerned with such activities, and therefore it is argued that tax exemptions for all organizations performing such work serve a public welfare purpose. Indeed, the efforts of private agencies, religious or not, save the government the expense of providing these services. . . .

This line of argument, however, cuts two ways. If churches enjoy the same tax exemption on secular activities as other private agencies, they must also be prepared to forsake special exemptions when they engage in business activities unrelated to their religions or eleemosynary mission. The delegates to the first National Study Conference on Church and. State sponsored by the National Council of Churches, February 4 to 7, 1964, accepted the logic of the conclusion when they expressed disapproval of exempting the unrelated taxable business income of church bodies. Neutrality implies no special privileges as well as no special burdens for religion.

Moreover, the "secular purpose" argument has limitations. While a secular purpose can be found in many of the secular activities and institutions of the churches, what justification is there for governmental support of houses of worship and of religious functions in a strict sense?

The answer to this question lies perhaps in the theory of religious neutrality formulated by Professor Wilber Katz of the University of Wisconsin. Professor Katz believes that the two religion clauses of the First Amendment should be read together as intended to promote a single purpose: the religious freedom of all citizens. Ordinarily, legislation serving a secular purpose will not run afoul of the establishment clause

(by favoring religion against nonreligion or one sect over another) or of the free exercise clause (by impairing a citizen's
freedom to practice his religion). There are certain cases,
however, where a too rigid interpretation of the establishment clause could lead to an interference with religious freedom guaranteed by the free exercise clause. Therefore he
reasons that legislatures should have at least discretionary
power to create exemptions to laws having this effect. The
result of such exemptions is not to prefer religion but rather
to safeguard the religious freedom of all citizens. . . .

Support for the constitutionality of religious tax exemptions is also found in the fact that they have such a long
history in this country. . . .

On the balance, it seems that a persuasive case for many
religious tax exemptions can be constructed. Only the Supreme Court, of course, can decide the issue. It is important,
however, that a climate of free and open debate on the issue
be maintained until the Court has been presented with the
proper case for resolving the issue. It would be dangerous for
private citizens or public officials to reach final opinions
about the issue prematurely, as President Kennedy seemed to
do in declaring federal aid to parochial schools unconstitu-
tional in the face of strong legal opinion to the contrary.
Indeed, the fact that the Supreme Court has twice declined
to pass on the issue may foreshadow the result of any future
tests of the constitutionality of the religious tax exemption.
Perhaps, as University of Michigan Law Professor Paul
Kauper observes, the court is disposed to accept Justice
Holmes's axiom that a page of history is worth a volume of
logic.